'When you meet a man who talks like that you should run for your life.'

Fifth victim's brother

'He is our dearest treasure on earth and we commit him to the God of all Graces.'

John Haigh's parents

John George Haigh. (Dunboyne, Lord (ed.), *Trial of John George Haigh*)

On what was to be her last day on earth, Mrs Olive Durand-Deacon sat down for breakfast as usual at eight o'clock at the Onslow Court Hotel, South Kensington. It was Friday, 18 February 1949 and the widowed Olive, who would have been 70 the following year, had been living at the Onslow Court, a residential hotel for the wealthy retired, for the last six years. The loneliness and shock of finding herself a widow at the age of 54 was partly tempered by her holding stocks and shares worth £36,000 (nearly £900,000 today). The companionship of her new friends and fellow residents at the hotel, particularly Mrs Constance Lane, who sat at the table in the dining room to her left, and Mr John Haigh, who sat at the table to her right – a comparative newcomer as he'd only lived at the hotel for the last four years – was also a comfort.

The only thing unusual today was John Haigh's empty table. Admittedly, he had to come down from his room on the fourth floor but as a rule he was there before Olive, ready to do 'his rounds', as he called his business trips. She was concerned about this and hoped he hadn't been taken ill in the night. Although he was a young man of 40 she thought he overdid it, careering around the country in his lovely Alvis motor car, and he sometimes looked quite worn out in the evenings when they sat down to dinner.

But, however tired John might be, there was always a smile on his face and time to exchange pleasantries about the day. Olive was surprised that a catch like him hadn't been snatched up years ago by some lucky girl and spirited off to a leafy suburb in the home counties. He did occasionally bring in a girl, whom he called Barbara, for afternoon tea, but as nice as she was she seemed young enough to be his daughter. He hinted to Olive over coffee one evening at the hotel that there had been a wife at some stage but never said more than that.

Sometimes there'd even be a little 'prize' for Olive or one of the other good ladies in the form of a piece of jewellery or bottle of perfume, something they couldn't get with rationing still in force after the war. They came at a price, of course, like the lovely crocodile handbag he'd brought her a year ago, charging only a modest £10 when in the shops it would be a lot more, if you could get something of such quality at all. And there was the exquisite blue sapphire and diamond ring she wore without ever telling a soul how much she paid John for it.

Then, to her relief, she spotted him on the other side of the dining room, stopping at a table and pulling out a long box with a watch or necklace wrapped in tissue. The expression of sheer delight on the face of the lady on the receiving end said it all, and she was gazing up at him and mouthing a question at which John was shrugging his shoulders and smiling his usual wonderful smile.

Perhaps if Olive were thirty years younger she might have designs on John herself, but at the age of 69 all that was over now and so what was the point; John Haigh, with his slightly high voice and petit bourgeois manners, would not be suitable for Olive Durand-Deacon, the widow of an army officer, in any case. But whatever you said about John, he did bring a lot of happiness to everyone at the hotel, and she for one wouldn't hear a word against him.

'Ah, Olive, good morning,' he greeted her as he passed her table, almost as if he were surprised to see her despite going through this ceremony every morning.

'Good morning, John, looking after us all as usual I see,' she replied with a regal nod of the head. People said she looked like Queen Elizabeth, who with her husband King George had looked after them so well during the war. Although not a vain woman, Olive liked to think she at least dressed like the queen and, while twenty years older, agreed that, well, there was something a little royal about her.

John hesitated before sitting down at his table. 'We must talk about your nails today, Olive,' he said.

'It would be a pleasure,' she replied, beaming.

She looked back at him as he poured his coffee and spread a piece of toast. Her examination of him was no intrusion because the single tables in the dining room at the Onslow Court were arranged and angled each on four tiles of floor space, like pieces on a chessboard, to maintain at least the pretence of privacy. The hotel was perfect for them, near the Science Museums and the Victoria and Albert, Harrods and the shops, and of course the Royal Albert Hall at the top of Queen's Gate for concerts.

Olive still worried about John even though he was now safely eating his breakfast. Despite wearing his usual immaculate suit, white shirt and silk tie, he looked weary and a little beaten. The hair was oiled and carefully brushed back and he was clean-shaven apart from his small moustache – the waft of Brylcreem and aftershave hit you as he passed. But there were bags under the piercing blue eyes and his effusive manner had gone over the last week – it was Friday and she hoped he would be more himself over the weekend.

Whatever was on his mind that morning, John was deep in thought until he'd finished his second piece of toast and drunk his second cup of coffee. Then he came over to Olive's table and pulled up a chair to sit beside her. He put his hand over hers on the pristine white tablecloth and patted her ringed fingers, something he'd never done in all the time they'd known each other. 'Now Olive,' he crooned, 'we have business to do and I have everything planned for you.'

But if she'd had an inkling of what John was planning for her that Friday afternoon, Olive would have run for her life.

John really had arranged everything, down to the last nail. The business they were discussing was the manufacture of artificial fingernails. Olive Durand-Deacon had a box full of them in her room, and when she heard that John was an inventor and the director of a light engineering company, she asked if he might be interested in a little business venture: he could manufacture the nails and she could design and market them.

He'd told her about the machine he wanted to market that threaded cotton through needles and a wonderful toy fort where all the soldiers moved around on a pulley system. She'd bought a couple of his handheld electric fans, but these had gone wrong rather soon, which embarrassed her because she'd bought two more and given them to friends going to Australia on a new ship, and she hoped these hadn't suffered the same fate.

But the fingernails were all her idea after she'd cut out pieces of newspaper and laid them to be painted on her own nails. While her marriage to a war hero with the Military Cross had been varied and fulfilling, she always harboured the idea that at heart she was a businesswoman. With the Second World War now four years behind them, women were starting to think how they looked again, about luxuries like decent hair and nails.

And John Haigh, despite the expensive cars, the suits and the silk ties, and despite, as he told her, being a solicitor specialising in probate matters in a past life, could himself do with a new business venture right now. Because, not for the first time in his life, he was financially embarrassed or, to put it less kindly, flat broke, down on his uppers, skint – however you wanted to describe it.

No one in the hotel knew about this, except the manageress, Mrs Alicia Robbie. She'd had to remind him no less than twice in the last week that he owed the hotel nearly £50 in bills and that if he didn't find the money within another week then he would have to leave. She was sorry to tell him this but it was hotel policy and this was not the first time she had had to speak to him and, after all, his room, a single on the fourth floor, was cheaper than the doubles on the lower floors like Mrs Durand-Deacon's. Mrs Robbie even had to send her head cashier up to his room to ask for the money, but John said he was unwell and would have to let them have it in a few days. To make matters worse, he'd earlier written the hotel a cheque that had been returned marked 'refer to drawer' by the bank.

Then there was the matter of his bank overdraft that came to £83 5s 10d, which was why they were refusing his cheques and, as the debt was unsecured, becoming more strident in their demands for repayment. His gambling had left him with a total of £352 (£8,700 today) owed to five different commission agencies.

And so at the beginning of the week, on Monday, 14 February 1949, Valentine's Day, John Haigh started to put his plan into place. Olive had Mrs Birin, Assistant Secretary of the Francis Bacon Society of which Olive was a member and who accompanied Olive to meetings at the Society and Foyle's literary luncheons, as her regular Monday lunch guest at the hotel. Among other things, the society supported the idea that Francis Bacon wrote Shakespeare's works for him, as Olive would remind John when they had a literary chat.

But the conversation today was more prosaic as Olive produced her box of plastic fingernails and, excusing herself to her guest, turned to John at the next table to show him.

John was sifting through the box like a pirate with a chest full of silver. 'Now, Olive,' he said to her. 'I've told them down at the factory about the plans and they can't wait to meet you. I shall whisk you down to Sussex later in the week for a look at some prototypes.'

Olive peered into the box. 'I've more upstairs. But I thought if I helped with the designs, then you could make them. I've even a few thoughts as to where we sell them. Oh, John, do you think this could really work?'

John sat back in his chair and raised his eyes to the ceiling. 'Work? I'll say this could work. We're tapping a market, Olive, and this is what it's all about,' he replied, tapping the side of his nose in what Olive thought rather a vulgar gesture.

She looked over her shoulder to see if her guest was listening, but she was busy tackling her chop.

'In fact,' added John, putting his head nearer hers, 'we are so impressed with the project we have decided that we should go halves with you on the funding. Only, my dear Olive, this is all between us and to go no further.'

'Of course, mum's the word,' said Olive, before he could tap his nose again.

The factory that John referred to was that of Hurstlea Products Ltd in West Street, Crawley. This light engineering business had been built up by his friend, Edward Jones, from humbler beginnings not far away in a one-up, one-down building in Leopold Road, which had been kept on as a storehouse since the move in 1947. In the same year, John was doing some experimental work with Edward on the gadget for threading needles, and John had even put up £200 towards the expenses of the project. He saw the invention as a real help to the blind but didn't say how this would help with the rest of their sewing. But John was exaggerating when he called himself a co-director of the firm; in fact, Edward had only offered him a directorship as a security against the money John had put down. Nothing had come of it and the matter had been forgotten, as presumably had the gadget for threading needles.

Nevertheless, John kept on a loose business relationship with Edward in acting as the firm's representative outside Crawley and in London generally. This was unpaid, but in return John had use of the storeroom in Leopold Road as a workshop more or less when he wanted to use it.

It was also an exaggeration that Edward Jones was relishing the prospect of manufacturing fingernails. John, who'd only seriously considered pressing ahead with the idea that morning – as he got out of bed, to be precise – had not even mentioned it to Edward yet.

On the following morning, Tuesday 15 February, Haigh motored down from Kensington to Crawley in the Alvis to the West Street factory before lunch. He parked the car, donned his long winter coat and marched into the factory looking more like a city stockbroker than an engineer.

By contrast Jones was sitting in his small office at his desk, dressed in a beige lab coat, with his head in his hands.

John put his head round the office door. 'Just popped in for the Leopold Road keys, Edward. Time for a quick chat?' he asked.

'Not really, John. I'm having a bloody awful day,' Jones replied.

John took no notice and sat himself down at the desk facing his colleague. 'Anything I can do?' he asked breezily.

'Got to lay off a few of the lads. I should have done it before Christmas.'

John unbuttoned his coat and put his hands on his hips. 'Well, times are tough for us all. In fact I was going to touch you for a little subbie, Edward.'

'How little?' Jones asked suspiciously. 'Not a good time of the year, John.'

'No, I know all that. But the fact is I've got caught short with hotel bills and the bank and that sort of thing,' replied John.

'I can't understand why you have to live in a posh London hotel and drive that car when most us mortals live down here and ride a bike.'

'Ah, but remember I'm the one who gets around town flying the flag, Edward. Customers expect it, you know. The car, the suit and tie, I'm worth a few orders to Hurstlea.'

'I know, I know. Anyway, how much do you want?'

'Fifty quid would do nicely. I can pay the hotel and give the bank something to keep them happy.'

Jones went over to an ancient safe in the corner and proceeded to open it with a key on the end of a chain. 'Alright, but I need it back by the end of the week. That's all the time I can give you, John, it's money I've put aside for a policy. I need it back Friday at the latest.'

'You're a scholar and a gentleman, Edward,' said John, taking the wad of notes and shoving it in his pocket. 'Now, there's another thing.'

'Quickly, John, please. I'm hungry and still putting off seeing these people.'

'No, this is a good one. This could make us a decent bit of money.'

'Like the needle threader?'

'That could still work to my mind, but after a war nobody wants to shell out money for a gadget on a job they can do themselves. No, what they want, what the ladies want, is a bit of luxury, especially when they've been breaking their nails in factories and farms, bless them. So we make them for them,' said John, pulling his chair up nearer the desk.

'Make what exactly?' asked Jones doubtfully.

'Fingernails. We make plastic fingernails to fit over the broken ones.'

Jones shook his head. 'Too costly, I'd say.'

'But we sell them for whatever we want to ask. I've a client lined up to come in on the scheme, loaded with money and raring to go,' said John, his blue eyes lighting up like Father Christmas producing a toy from his sack.

Jones sat back in his chair, opened a drawer and produced a sandwich in greaseproof paper. 'Sorry, John, not interested,' he said, unwrapping the sandwich.

'Well, I said I'd bring them down to the factory later in the week. They might put up some money.'

Jones bit off the end of his sandwich and threw it back down on the wrapper. 'Not here, I'm afraid, I've got enough troubles to have to worry about fingernails.'

The breath ran out of John in a long sigh. He shook his head but accepted the offer of sharing his colleague's lunch, and so over spam sandwiches with mustard, and a thermos flask of weak tea, both made earlier that morning by Mrs Jones for her husband while John Haigh slept in silk pyjamas in the Onslow Court Hotel, Olive Durand-Deacon's fate was sealed.

3

Next morning a smiling and more assured John Haigh phoned down from his room in the hotel to the manageress to say he was now in a position to deal with his bill if she would care to come up to discuss the matter. In fact, she said didn't care to go up to his room to discuss this or anything else as she felt she'd chased around after him enough as it was. She sent her cashier, Mrs Kirkwood, up instead, expecting more excuses and delays about payment.

Mrs Kirkwood found him sitting in his armchair, doing the crossword.

'My word, Mrs Kirkwood, you look terrific this morning,' he greeted her.

'Does that mean you can't pay?' she asked.

'Not a bit of it, not a bit,' he said, standing up and throwing the newspaper down on the unmade bed. 'It was a complete error by my bank to return my cheque the other day. I can tell you I've given them a piece of my mind and been assured heads will roll. Now, I can give you the choice, cash or a cheque?'

'Cash, please, Mr Haigh,' said Mrs Kirkwood, still waiting for the catch.

'Very well,' he said and walked over to his desk. He opened the drawer and produced the borrowed wad of notes, which he placed disdainfully on the bed like dirty linen for the laundry. 'Take what you need from that,' he added and went back to his crossword.

As Mrs Kirkwood carefully counted out the first £32 10s to cover the returned cheque, John looked up from his crossword. 'Rubbish in the Far East,' he announced.

'I'm sorry?'

'Rubbish in the Far East. Four letters.'

Mrs Kirkwood ignored the question and finished her counting. 'Then there's another seventeen pounds and ten shillings to bring us up to date, if you please.'

'That'll have to be a cheque in another week.'

'No, the arrangement is that you pay up the full amount, Mr Haigh, and I will not take a cheque,' said Mrs Kirkwood firmly.

This time it was Mrs Kirkwood who didn't wait for a reply, and she went on counting the notes to the full £50.

'Now, I have a present for you to make up for all the inconvenience,' said John with a change of tone, reaching under his bed and producing a bottle of sherry when the counting ended.

'Thank you, Mr Haigh, but I don't drink.'

'For Mr Kirkwood, then.'

She hesitated for a moment, looking at the label on the bottle. 'Well, it is his favourite, as a matter of fact.'

'I thought it might be.'

'Who told you?'

'You, Mrs Kirkwood, on several occasions, before times were so choppy, when the seas ran calmer between us. Now please take it and I can do my rounds.'

John saw her to the door, which he opened for her. 'Junk,' he said as she passed him.

'I beg your pardon?'

'Rubbish in the Far East – junk,' he repeated and gave her a thumbs up before closing the door after her.

John Haigh's rounds that morning once again centred on Crawley, with a visit first to Northgate Road where he collected Tom Davies, a welding engineer who did occasional jobs for him, and took him over to the Leopold Road workshop. 'I want you to pick up some acid for me,' John explained on the way over. 'You'll need an empty carboy.'

Inside the workshop were three carboys – large glass containers capable of holding 10gal of corrosive liquid – each containing different levels of concentrated acid. With an effort, the two men emptied the contents of one carboy into the other two.

'You'll also need this,' said John, handing Tom a printed order for the supply of one container of commercial sulphuric acid from the technical liaison officer of Onslow Court, SW7.

Tom looked at the order and turned it over in his hand. 'Who's this technical liaison officer, then?' he asked.

'Me, old chap,' replied John, slapping him on the back, flashing a smile and pushing a couple of pound notes into his hand. 'See you tomorrow, and don't drink any of it on the way.'

With the full carboy safely delivered the next day, which was Thursday, John ordered and collected a black drum from a firm of chemical merchants in Barking. However, on getting it back to the Leopold Road workshop he decided it was not corrosive resistant and so drove back to Barking to exchange it for a green one specially prepared to resist acids. In fact the suppliers of the drum said the lining was of such a quality you could keep your soup or beer in it.

This extra and unforeseen trip to Barking only just gave John time to get back to the West Street factory before five o'clock. Having at last got round to telling his workers the bad news about redundancies, Edward Jones was in no mood for conversation.

John could see the mood he was in the moment he entered the building. 'Sorry, Edward, but it's one more quick favour I need,' he said and produced a brand new stirrup pump, which he placed on the bench in front of them.

'I don't want to buy it, if that's what you're asking,' said Jones, picking it up and inspecting it cautiously.

'No, I wondered if you could saw the foot off it for me.'

Jones, aware of John's inability to handle tools, offered to do the job by removing two rivets to allow the metal stirrup to come off.

The foot fell on to the floor with a clatter and Jones picked it up and gave it to John. 'If that's all you want, John, then good afternoon, but I'd appreciate some help shifting some metal sheets out of Leopold Road tomorrow morning,' said Jones brusquely.

John gave him the foot back. 'You can have that for doing it,' he replied.

Jones threw the part under the bench and went back to work.

John left the building satisfied everything was now ready for tomorrow's meeting, supposedly to discuss the manufacture and marketing of plastic fingernails, with Olive Durand-Deacon.

The next day was Friday, 18 February and the morning on which John Haigh had arrived late for breakfast, stopping afterwards at Olive Durand-Deacon's table to confirm he hadn't forgotten their business meeting.

In fact, he'd thought about little else for the past few days as the debts swam in like ducks in a row. The reason he was late for breakfast was that he'd been sitting in his armchair up in his room, wondering if the better option still wouldn't be to ask Olive to fund the project with cash up front. She was a wealthy woman and this would put him in immediate funds to pay his debts, but without the support of Edward and the factory she would soon twig nothing further was happening and start asking questions.

Before he left her after breakfast, John suggested they meet at the hotel reception after lunch, say at 2.15 if that suited her, and they could drive down to Crawley to look at the specimen plastic sheets he'd got that might act as a prototype for the project. That was the word, prototype.

First John drove alone down to Crawley to help Edward move the metal sheets out of Leopold Street over to the West Street factory. He would let it drop that he might be bringing someone down to discuss the fingernails in the afternoon, but he wouldn't say much more. This would just about give him time to get back to Kensington for lunch and pick up Olive for the return trip back to Crawley in the afternoon.

But just as he'd left the dining room after breakfast, Mrs Constance Lane leant over from her table to ask Olive if she might be interested in shopping and lunch that morning in Kensington. Olive gracefully declined the invitation, explaining she was going down to see John Haigh's factory. Mrs Lane had always kept her distance from Mr Haigh, whom she thought too young and too smooth – and to be honest, too sharp – to be living in a residential hotel like the Onslow with a lot of women twice his age. On more than one occasion she'd said to Olive that if you opened Mr Haigh's coat you would probably find it lined with watches and the other jewellery he brought into the hotel. For Constance it was the height of vulgarity that a resident should be selling what must be black market goods actually in the hotel; if Haigh wasn't so thick with Olive, she would have had a word with Mrs Robbie, the manageress, by now. Olive thought this very amusing and told Constance she was jealous.

However, there wasn't a lot left in Olive's day that Friday to be jealous about.

The two-hour drive to Crawley left Olive wanting to spend a penny, and John suggested they use the cloakroom at the George Hotel in the High Street as there weren't any facilities in the workshop, as he now started to call it instead of 'the factory'. When they reached the building in Leopold Road Olive was taken aback at how modest it was: it was hardly a factory by any stretch of the imagination. However, John was now explaining that this was the workroom that he used to design and build prototypes and that the main factory was over in West Street.

John parked the car in the yard outside, near the door to the building, and unloaded a black hatbox and briefcase from the boot. The yard was full of debris and lumber was propped up against the side of the building as Olive, dressed in her black Persian lamb coat, red handbag and jewellery more suitable for an evening at the theatre, followed him to the door.

Inside the building the scene wasn't much more reassuring. It was cold and damp. A large workbench with a clutter of tools lay under the front window and along one wall. A rubber apron hung neatly on the back wall, and on the floor were arranged a large green drum and carboys packed in straw. An acrid smell filled the place. Olive couldn't quite say what it was, but it reminded her of cleaning kitchens and bathrooms in the days when she had to clean kitchens and bathrooms.

John put the hatbox on the floor and left it there, open, near the bench. He took off his camelhair coat and hung it carefully behind the door. 'I'll keep mine on, if you don't mind,' said Olive, starting to shiver.

'We'll soon have things warmed up for you,' John replied, blowing into his hands and rubbing them together. 'Now, to business. I want first to show you the prototype for the nails and see what you think of the colours.'

With this he produced two red cellophane sheets from the briefcase and placed them in front of Olive on the bench. As she bent down to look at them, he reached into the hat box and pulled out a revolver. As Olive was about to say she thought the colour was alright but the sheets looked a little insubstantial, John brought the revolver up behind her neck and shot her with a single shot through the back of the head.

Fourteen stone of Mrs Durand-Deacon crashed to the ground in a black ball of Persian lamb and lay there motionless. John knelt to extract a wad of cotton wool from his black case with the professionalism of a doctor treating a casualty, and held it to the wound in her head to staunch the flow of blood. Death had been instantaneous, and he was glad of this because he didn't like hurting anyone.

Then he took off his victim's fur coat, in case it got any blood on it, and hung it over his on the back of the door. He'd get the coat cleaned and in a good state to sell.

Next he bent down to unscrew Olive's earrings, pulled the rings off her fingers and dropped them all into his jacket pocket. Then it was the turn of bracelets, the crucifix around her neck and finally the watch from the still warm wrist. All this jewellery would raise some immediate cash, and the rest of it, her properties and various capital assets, he would transfer later into his own name. Her red handbag didn't have much to offer except for 30s in notes and some loose change, and all this he stuffed into his pocket, keeping a mental note of what the tally might be. A few bits and pieces he thought he might keep, like her pen now he could start writing cheques again. Finally he threw the empty handbag into the green drum.

Then, without returning to the body, John put his coat back on and drove over to the West Street factory where he found an exhausted Edward Jones doing some paperwork at his desk. One or two workers were whistling and clearing up their benches. 'Glad it's the weekend, eh, Edward?' asked John, without a hint of anything else on his mind.

Jones looked up. 'Oh, it's you, John. Yes, very glad as a matter of fact. What a week,' he said and immediately looked down again at his desk, making it clear he didn't want a conversation.

'Just thought I'd tell you they didn't turn up,' said John.

'Who didn't turn up?'

'The people interested in the fingernails. They didn't show,' said John.

'Well, the end to a perfect bloody week, then,' said Jones, without the energy to even remind John about the money he'd lent him.

For John it was the end to a perfect bloody week. It was perfect, it was bloody and it was the answer to his problems. Now he could deal with Olive's body in his own time, and arriving back at the storehouse he took off his coat and jacket and, with several pieces of electric flex that had been hanging untidily on the wall for too long, strapped the arms up tight against Olive's sides and then the knees up to her chest, like a turkey ready for the oven. As he did so her skirt fell immodestly down to her thighs and he pulled it back up and tucked it under her knees, thankful he was not the type of person who might have taken advantage of a woman in a vulnerable position. He'd had a strict Plymouth Brethren upbringing to thank for that and parents who showed him the difference between right and wrong. He hadn't even touched his young friend Barbara inappropriately in the five years he'd known her for the same reason, not a finger.

Next he lay the green drum on its side on the floor with the open end facing the body, and with a lot of difficulty pushed and shoved the 14-stone deadweight head first into the drum, which was only just wide enough to take the body. With a final heave he pulled the drum upright.

Sweating and short of breath, he decided he needed fortifying with a bit of tea before he finished the job. It was about six o'clock and he could hear someone outside draw up at the gates of the yard and open a vehicle door. Time to get the equipment off and put away and put some of these things back into the boot of the car. As John put his jacket and coat back on he could see the removal van belonging to the firm they shared the yard with coming in to park for the night. He carried on and put the hatbox and briefcase, together with the jewellery and Persian lamb coat, back in the car.

His feeling of relief now turning to exultation, he drove to Ye Olde Priors Restaurant in The Square, Crawley, for an egg on toast with a cup of tea.

The proprietor, Mr Outram, knew him by sight. 'Glad it's the end of the week?' he asked.

'I've got a long drive yet up to Kensington,' replied John.

'Well, that's alright for a youngster like you,' said Mr Outram, serving the egg on toast.

John laughed for the first time that afternoon. 'I like the youngster bit – I'm thirty-eight, you know.'

'Then you can't be married,' said Mr Outram, and as he said it John remembered he *was* still married, even though he hadn't seen his wife for ten years. He'd mentioned this to Barbara now she was twenty and starting to talk about marriage and she for her part didn't seem very concerned about it. She trusted him to get a divorce when the time came.

He didn't know what made him think of it, but John suddenly remembered Olive, who was a bit of a reader, telling him about a Russian novel where the murderer plans every detail of the murder and then forgets to lock the door. In the first fit of anything approaching panic that afternoon, John couldn't now remember locking the workshop door when he left.

He paid his bill quickly and drove back to the yard, where sure enough he found the door to the workshop unlocked – but there wasn't a soul around and his secret was safe.

He went to the back of the room, put on a raincoat and donned the rubber apron, tying it at the back like a housewife about to cook the Sunday roast. From the hatbox he produced a war surplus gas mask and placed it over his head, with the respirator in a bag hanging over his chest. Finally came long-sleeved industrial gloves and boots before he felt sufficiently protected to use the stirrup pump.

With the foot of the pump removed the previous day by Edward, the neck of the pump could now be inserted into the top of the first carboy to allow the sulphuric acid to be transferred into the drum. As the drum filled, the acid got to work on first the clothes, then the flesh and bones of the body until the whole mixture was starting to warm in a bubbling froth. Soon the drum would be too hot to touch, and with the contents of the carboy pumped into it John started to relax for the first time.

Everything in the drum was cooking nicely, and he used a wooden stick to give things a stir. Some fat bubbled to the surface of the stew and he reckoned the weekend would probably give it enough time to complete the job and reduce it all to a sludge that could be tipped out into the yard.

This time John remembered, when he finally left the building, to lock the door behind him, safe in the knowledge that no one else would get in over the weekend as he had the keys in his pocket.

Before driving back to London he thought he'd treat himself to a proper dinner at the George Hotel, where earlier he and Olive had stopped to use the cloakroom. He ordered chicken with a decent wine, but the wine was too acidic and the chicken too fleshy.

Poor Olive, he reflected over brandy and a cigar, it had felt like he was disposing of his own mother.

Next morning at breakfast at the Onslow Court Hotel Mrs Constance Lane was a troubled woman. She sat at her table having her breakfast as usual, and Mr Haigh sat at his table having his breakfast as usual, but between them Mrs Durand-Deacon's table was conspicuously empty. This worried Mrs Lane all the more because last night Mrs Durand-Deacon's table was empty at dinner, and while her friend might not keep her up to date on her every move, it was unusual, to say the least, for Olive not to tell her that she was intending to be away overnight.

Then she was just starting her second cup of coffee when that ghastly little man Mr Haigh got up and actually came over to her table. She had barely ever spoken to him and had never understood Olive's friendship with a man who, with his rather overbearing optimism about everything and – let's be frank about it – barely disguised lower-middle-class manners, had seemed lately to monopolise Olive's time in the Tudor Room, discussing plans about manufacturing something as ridiculous as fingernails. Olive had been a force in her day with the suffragette movement, but with a services and professional background she was hardly schooled in the seedy world of business, and Constance just hoped it wasn't all going to end in tears or, even worse, with that second-hand car salesman Mr Haigh getting his hands on her money.

Mr Haigh came up to her table and put both his hands palm down on the tablecloth in an entirely inappropriate way for someone who didn't know her. He smelt of a dubious aftershave and his blue eyes reminded Constance of a Siamese cat she'd once owned that proved unreliable.

'Do you know anything about Mrs Durand-Deacon; is she ill?' he asked. 'Do you know where she is?'

Constance wanted to reply that if she did know where her friend was she certainly wouldn't tell him. 'No, I do not know where she is,' she replied.

Mr Haigh stood up and muttered something she couldn't hear. 'Well,' she added, 'do *you* not know where she is? I understood from her that you wanted to take her to your factory.'

For a moment Mr Haigh stopped smiling and the eyes lost their sparkle. Then the smile as quickly returned. 'Yes, that's right, but I wasn't ready. I hadn't had lunch and she said she wanted to go to the Army & Navy Stores, and she asked me to pick her up there.'

'I see,' said Constance.

'But I waited for her there for an hour and she didn't turn up,' added Mr Haigh.

This didn't sound like the organised Olive she knew at all – Constance might have believed it if Haigh hadn't turned up, but not Olive.

'Well, I must do something about it,' said Constance, not knowing really what to do, except the obvious like checking with the hotel management in case Olive had said something to them.

She walked with Mr Haigh to the door of the dining room, and as they entered the hallway it suddenly occurred to her that no one had thought of actually going and knocking on Olive's door. The poor woman might be in there stricken with some terrible illness or, even worse, lying dead on the floor after a heart attack.

Constance walked up the stairs to the first floor and along the corridor to Room 115, where she knocked melodramatically and put her ear to the door. She was about to knock again when a chambermaid appeared from over the corridor carrying a pile of sheets.

'Unlock the door,' Mrs Lane commanded, pulling herself up to her full 5ft.

'I'm sorry, madam?' replied the chambermaid, visibly shaken by the request.

'I believe my friend Mrs Durand-Deacon may be unwell and unable to answer the door.'

The chambermaid didn't need asking twice and unlocked the door. Mrs Lane pushed her aside and strode in. One look at the bed, on which the cover was folded neatly back and the lace nightdress laid out, told her it hadn't been slept in overnight.

There was a stillness about the room, like walking into a church on a weekday when nobody's there. Instead of incense there was the fragrance of Chanel and in place of the altar, a table with photos of a distinguished-looking husband, one of them with him standing outside Buckingham Palace holding his Military Cross, a younger and radiant Olive at his side.

'Well, I don't know,' muttered Mrs Lane, lowering her shoulders and returning to her slightly stooped posture, looking around for some sort of clue. The suitcase Olive used on the rare occasions she did stay away was sitting on top of her wardrobe, and a recently published biography of Francis Bacon lay on her bedside table with a half-filled glass of water.

Constance walked back down the stairs and told Mr Haigh. 'I don't know,' she repeated.

Mr Haigh did know, of course. He knew only too well, and it was now just a matter of time before the balloon went up.

Meanwhile he had Olive's jewellery and fur coat in the boot of the Alvis. It was time to do his rounds, to include checking how the patient herself was doing.

On his way to Crawley he stopped at Barrett's, the jewellers in Putney High Street, and sold Olive's watch for £10, giving a false name and address to be on the safe side. This was an encouraging start and put John in a good humour. In fact, with a good hotel breakfast inside him and with the story about having to wait unsuccessfully for Olive at the Army & Navy Stores proving once again that he could think on his feet, he felt almost invincible. It was all so easy – the Alvis purred like a cat, and behind him he had a boot full of jewellery that was going to keep him in cash for weeks. In fact – and the idea came to him in an epiphany – why not be the one to go and report Olive missing to the police himself? He would accompany Mrs Lane and she could do all the talking to those dimwits. Would anyone ever suspect a murderer going to the police to report his own victim missing?

However, at Crawley things were not all quite they might be. Inside the workroom the drum was still warm to touch, doing its work on what remained of Mrs Durand-Deacon, who was now reduced to a dark soup, but as John stirred the sludge with his stick he quickly realised there were pieces of fat and bone floating around in the mixture. For the first time he felt a little resentful of his old friend: why did she have to be so fat, especially after a war when food was still being rationed? And while she couldn't have anticipated the inconvenience she might cause him, was it really fair that she carried 4 stone too much when the rest of them were struggling with ration books?

He pushed a lump of fat down with his stick, but it stubbornly floated back to the surface. Well, another twenty-four hours might do it, but at worst he'd throw it out with the rest of the sludge and no one would notice in a yard already full of debris and bits of junk.

Then it was on to Horsham and a call at Bull's the jewellers with the bracelets and rings, but Mr Bull who did the valuing was out and John said he'd call again. There was no hurry and he knew he was going to get a decent amount for all of it.

Then it was back to town via Reigate, where at 'Cottage Cleaners' he presented the Persian lamb coat for cleaning. Not that Mrs Durand-Deacon didn't keep the coat immaculately – it still smelt of her Chanel – but it had taken a tumble on to a dirty floor and John wanted to get the proper price for the coat. He'd had a quick look at it in the workshop before he left for any bloodstains, but he couldn't see anything, and this is why he'd armed himself the day before with the cotton wool to avoid staining.

As John waited for the girl to complete the receipt, the smell of cleaning chemicals in the shop took him back to his own efforts to run a cleaning firm, which had been successful until his partner died in a road accident and his widow dissolved the partnership. Still, he'd found a more lucrative way of dissolving business partners now and he must concentrate on that.

The last stop on his rounds, something he couldn't see as really necessary but better to err on the side of caution, was to call in at the factory and make sure no one was getting funny about him keeping the keys to the workroom over the weekend. He decided to make the excuse of wanting to use the lavatory, and he made sure it was nearly four o'clock when he called, just before they finished early on a Saturday. At worst if Edward had wanted to use Leopold Road it would have been too late in the day. He saw Edward on the other side of the shop floor and gave him a cursory wave. Edward gave him a wave back without making any sign of wanting to speak to him. John pointed at the toilet door, gave a thumbs up and darted inside. When he emerged there was no sign of Edward and John made it back to the car, looking as if he had all the time in the world.

He drove sedately back to London, thankful not to be rushing to another deadline except for meeting Barbara as usual for Saturday afternoon tea, thankful to be solvent, able to have dinner tonight at the hotel and know he could pay for it.

If anyone ever started any moralising about all this, then he'd remind them Jesus didn't expect his disciples to work but rely on the people to feed and clothe them. This was the principle that he, John Haigh, had respected all his life and God had been kind to him, allowing him to carry out His work. This was how he intended to live the rest of his life and, if necessary, the next life, should he be sent there earlier than expected.

Since he'd moved into the Onslow Court Hotel four years ago, John Haigh had maintained his relationship with Barbara Stephens but at a distance. They would meet regularly on Saturdays and perhaps have afternoon tea at the hotel and walk up to the Royal Albert Hall for a concert or drive into the West End and, in Barbara's words, do a show.

Barbara was a pretty girl, half John's age; she was 20 now but only 15, in the bloom of youth, when they first met. Her father had business dealings with John and offered to put John up in the family home in Crawley temporarily when he was bombed out of his room in Queen's Gate Terrace. Barbara fell immediately for the suave looks and the charm, the sports car in which he whirled her off for rides and the sheer worldliness of the man. He taught her about his love of the arts, books, wine and music and started taking her to concerts. He advised her how to dress and talked about all the things boys of her age couldn't talk about – even sex, although John never once tried it on with her in all the years he knew her. On that front there was little intimacy, and Barbara saw this as respect for her and decided to wait until she was 21 for marriage. Although her parents were uneasy about them as a couple because of the difference in age, they could see John was her life and let it be. Like their daughter, they trusted him.

But even Barbara, looking through rose-coloured glasses, could see there was a part of John's life he kept to himself, saying little about where he spent his time and what he did for the rest of the week when he didn't see her. On one occasion he brought a trunk full of some smart clothes, expensive and nearly new, and offered to sell them to Barbara, her mother and sister, saying they belonged to friends who'd gone to live abroad. Barbara bought one item, a green dress.

On another occasion Barbara's father lent John his car to run a business errand and John, who was driving alone, rang to say he'd run into an army truck and written off both vehicles, probably due to his poor eyesight. He was lucky not to have been killed and walked away with hardly a scratch, offering to pay for the car, although the incident was never mentioned again. The accident only served to increase John's mystique in Barbara's eyes.

She was now blossoming into a mature 20-year-old woman and starting to think about marriage to John once she was 21, which she would be in April that year. She'd assumed that once she was 21 John would ask her to marry him. He'd even told her he was already married but hadn't seen his wife for many years, and she trusted him enough to know that he would divorce his wife when marriage for them was realistically on the horizon. Barbara had found secretarial work and was starting to save modest amounts for the day. John, for his part, never seemed short of money – rather the opposite in the way he lived with expensive hotels, meals out and luxury cars – although recently she felt he had been reining in rather on buying the best tickets and eating in the most expensive restaurants. Even Saturday teas at the hotel were reduced to a pot of tea and sandwich – without the scones and cakes.

But this Saturday afternoon things looked different from the moment Barbara walked into the hotel to meet John. He was waiting for her in reception and took her into the Tudor Room by the arm, sat her down and this time ordered the full works for tea. The shadows under his eyes had disappeared and there a new animated look about him.

Barbara noticed the way he ordered tea in the old cavalier, jokey manner. 'You're looking very pleased with yourself today,' she said.

'I should be,' he replied. 'A deal's come up and I'm feeling rich again.'

'Oh yes, anything interesting?'

'Just a conversion job, but I haven't done one of these for a few years and, well, you know how it is, you start to wonder if you've lost your touch,' said John, taking a moment to greet Mrs Lane as she passed with a friend on her way to tea.

'You've never said anything to her before, John.'

'Such a nice lady. That reminds me, she's a good friend of Mrs Durand-Deacon. I mentioned her in my letter this week. She's the one who wants us to go into business making fingernails. A very curious thing has happened. I was going to take her down to Crawley this week to the factory to talk about it with Edward but she didn't turn up and I had to go on without her.'

'I remember her. She was very elegant and very well off, you said.'

'That's the one. Anyway, it now seems she's disappeared. She didn't turn up for breakfast and her bed wasn't slept in last night. It's like something out of Agatha Christie. Mrs Lane wants to go and report it all to the police and make a real drama out of it, but you'll probably finds she trots in tonight saying she's been to visit someone in the family – they've got houses all over the country. Perhaps she's eloped, now that really would be something,' said John, unable to stop himself going into giggles.

He hadn't stopped giggling by the time the tea was brought, and after pouring the tea and offering Barbara a sandwich, he launched straight into the cakes and scones, awarding himself large dollops of cream like a schoolboy out for a half-term treat.

Barbara said as much as he came back to the sandwiches. 'It feels like a holiday today, with Christmas and a few birthdays rolled into one. The reason I asked you to come up a little early today was that I'm taking you on another little treat. I know you've never been, so get your coat on when you've finished your tea and we'll be off,' announced John.

Barbara was used to his little surprises by now. Often it was a trip down to Brighton in the Alvis, without warning, so that she felt she never had the right clothes, followed by fish and chips somewhere near the front and then back up in the evening to Crawley, where he would drop her off at her parents.

Today it was different. They got off the tube at Baker Street and then walked up the Marylebone Road to Madame Tussauds. 'There's only one part of this really worth seeing,' said John.

It was late afternoon and the queues had dwindled to a few families at the main doors determined to get their money's worth from their day in London. He paid for two tickets and took her by the hand down to the entrance of the Chamber of Horrors. 'Oh, John, do we have to?' Barbara protested.

Above the entrance the Count de Lorge peered out from behind bars during his thirty years' incarceration in the Bastille, looking down on the old toll bell from Newgate Prison that would be rung as prisoners passed from the prison to the gallows. 'Just a quick look, just to see who they've got in there,' said John.

They found Amelia Dyer, the baby farmer who murdered probably over 400 children and babies, and Dr Crippen, executed for the murder of his wife in 1910. There was George Joseph Smith, 'The Brides in the Bath' murderer, but what most fascinated John were the death masks made by Madame Tussaud herself during the French Revolution, including Marie Antoinette, Robespierre and Louis XVI.

'How do they make them?' asked Barbara, half appalled, half fascinated.

'Easy,' replied John, ever the engineer. 'You make a mask out of plaster from the head, let it set as your cast, fill it with molten wax and remove the cast. Rather like making an Easter egg.'

'I don't think I'd like to do that,' said Barbara.

'Better if you can do it from life,' said John thoughtfully. 'Then everyone's happy.'

One Frenchman was missing from this formidable list of compatriots, and that was Georges-Alexandre Sarret, executed in 1934 in Aix-en-Provence after murdering two victims in an insurance fraud and then disposing of their bodies in a bathtub filled with 26gal of sulphuric acid.

'Well, what do you think?' asked John when they'd finished their tour.

'I think it's all pretty horrible and I'd like to go home,' replied Barbara.

'Suppose, Barb, suppose I ended up in here one day, would you come and visit me?'

Barbara shuddered. 'Now you're trying to frighten me. I know you, and you wouldn't hurt a fly. That's why I love you.'

But Barbara didn't know him, and he would hurt a fly – several flies, in fact – if it kept him in the Onslow Court Hotel and out of debt. That was her last date with John – the following Saturday he unusually hadn't got in touch with her during the week to fix up their weekend meeting, and when she phoned him at the hotel he simply said he was 'too busy', in a way so distant and disinterested she knew something was wrong.

The next morning the breakfast scene in the hotel was repeated, with Mrs Lane seated on one side of an empty table and John Haigh on the other, only today was Sunday and breakfast was served an hour later to allow the staff a lie-in and the residents to go to early communion at St Augustine's up the road and not miss breakfast. Constance Lane did her best not to catch Mr Haigh's eye – it was bad enough having all this worry about Olive without having to deal with him and his sudden interest in her dear friend. So at the end of the meal she left her table without looking up and made for the Tudor Room, where she usually read the Sunday papers, although today it would be hard concentrating on anything very much.

She'd hardly sat down and taken up one of the papers – in which she had no interest but simply picked up to look occupied – when over the top of her paper arose, like the dawn of the Apocalypse, the smiling face of John George Haigh.

'Mrs Lane, I hate to disturb you again after your breakfast, but I must ask if you have heard anything of Mrs Durand-Deacon,' he asked.

'I'm afraid not, Mr Haigh. I am going to have to report it,' she replied.

'I think we should go together to Chelsea Police Station.'

'I think so too.'

'I will drive you there, if I may,' he said, and they agreed that if there was no news by lunch then they would meet at reception at 2.15 and he would drive her there – exactly forty-eight hours after John had picked up Olive on Friday to drive her down to Crawley.

It must have been the memories of driving Olive down to Crawley that made John think of what he'd do if Mrs Lane wanted to spend a penny, and then of course he realised she could use the facilities in the police station rather than have to worry about using the cloakroom in the George at Crawley. The strain of trying to make conversation with Mrs Lane, who was largely silent during the trip, kept John thinking of how he might have to dispose of her. How would he take her down to Crawley if he had to? Was she interested in making fingernails, a gadget that threaded needles or anything that would provide an excuse to get her down there to look at a prototype? But then he dismissed the idea quickly: two residents missing from the Onslow Court would look like more than coincidence.

At the police station Constance Lane once again drew herself up to her full 5ft as she approached the desk sergeant, but even then her chin barely rose above the counter. 'Good afternoon, officer, I wish to report a missing person, if I may,' she announced.

'You may, madam. Would that missing person be a female or male?' he asked.

'It's my friend, you understand, just disappeared,' said Constance, not quite taking in the question.

The sergeant put down his pen and looked up at her with an expression that asked not to make his life more difficult than it already was. 'Female,' added Constance.

'In that case I'm going to hand you over to my colleague Sergeant Lambourne,' said the officer and disappeared to emerge at a side door and beckon them into a small interview room.

Sergeant Lambourne, a no-nonsense police officer in her mid-thirties with a keener, more intelligent face than the desk sergeant, appeared to complete a report sheet, on to which she wrote copious notes summarising what Constance had to say about how long she'd known Olive, how Olive would spend her time and how often and for how long she stayed away from the hotel.

Sergeant Lambourne then turned to Constance's companion. 'And you, sir, you're a resident of the hotel, I understand. Do you have a special association with Mrs Durand-Deacon?' she asked.

John sat back in his chair and laughed with a short snort. 'Good gracious no, she's old enough to be my mother.'

Sergeant Lambourne wasn't smiling. 'I didn't meant it quite like that, sir. But I take it you don't know her quite as well as Mrs Lane.'

John sat back up. 'As a matter of fact, we do have a special association in that we have a business project together.'

'What sort of business project is that?'

'The manufacture of artificial fingernails. I'm the co-director of a civil engineering company. My co-director isn't so keen on the idea, but I think it could work.'

Sergeant Lambourne scribbled a few more notes on her sheet. 'You both tell me Mrs Durand-Deacon is an active woman, so might it be quite possible that she's gone away for a day or two?' she asked.

'She wouldn't go away without telling me, or the hotel management. It's not a hotel in that sense, it's more like our home. We're all retired, you see,' said Constance.

The sergeant turned to John. 'All retired except for you, Mr Haigh,' she said slowly.

'Someone's got to keep them in order,' said John and, when this produced no reaction, he winked and added, 'I keep them young, you see, sergeant.'

Sergeant Lambourne saw them out of the building and went back to the interview room to pick up her papers. From the window in the corridor she saw Mrs Lane and John making their way up Lucan Place to their car. John had taken the arm of his companion, and for all purposes the couple looked like mother and dutiful son out for a Sunday walk.

As she watched him open the passenger door and steer her into the seat, chatting to her as he folded the hem of her dress so as not to catch it in the door, still smiling and cracking some joke, Sergeant Lambourne instinctively knew something was wrong. Why was a man with Haigh's charm and confidence, and apparent wealth looking at the car, living in what sounded like a retirement home for the elderly, with a bunch of old biddies thirty years his senior?

She didn't like it – and she didn't like him very much. He didn't fit. But whether this all had anything to do with the missing resident from the hotel was an entirely different matter. She was about to go off duty and go home, but instead she typed up her report sheet – she did all her own typing so it would have to be done anyway – and then, putting on her coat and hat, hesitated a moment before making her way to her boss's office.

She hesitated because it was Sunday and she knew Detective Inspector Shelly Symes, Head of CID for West London, was only in the building working on a major investigation that hadn't given him much time off in the last two weeks.

She knocked twice and poked her head around the door. 'I'm sorry, sir, I was just going off-duty but I wondered if I could have a quick word. I know you're busy,' she said.

'Busy achieving nothing, Sergeant, that's all. Come in,' said Symes.

Symes was a large man, sitting in a large swivel chair that creaked every time he moved. He looked more like a theatre impresario than a police officer and would have looked equally at home sitting behind a desk in Tin Pan Alley with a cigar in his mouth. His desk now was full of papers and empty coffee cups. He was making longhand notes using a fountain pen with a broken clip.

'The thing is, sir, I've just done a first report on a missing person. She's a resident at the Onslow Court Hotel and no one's seen her in the last forty-eight hours.'

'The Onslow Court in Queen's Gate – mostly for the wealthy retired.'

'That's the one. One of this lady's friends came to report it, a Mrs Lane, accompanied by a gentleman who is also a resident, a Mr Haigh. I've come to ask if we could run a crime record on him,' said Sergeant Lambourne.

DI Symes relit his pipe and threw the match into a metal waste bin. 'What's the matter with him – bit past it to be running any sort of racket, isn't he?'

'That's the thing, sir. He's younger than the rest of them, most of the residents that is, by thirty years or so.'

'And most of them are women up there, aren't they?'

'I imagine they are. I'll go up there tomorrow after I've checked the hospitals for our missing lady. Haigh's nearly 40 and a bit pleased with himself. He's wrong, if you see what I mean, sir.'

'Sounds just your type, Sergeant. Okay, I'll ask records to run a check on him. But this might all make more sense when you get up there to the hotel tomorrow.'

'Thank you, sir.'

'Call it a woman's intuition, shall we? We've seen it work for you before, haven't we?' said Symes.

He looked at his watch and said he'd give her a lift home so that they could have what was left of their Sunday with their families.

From the moment she got back into the office next morning Sergeant Lambourne wasted no time. She telephoned the local hospitals, ambulance stations and surgeries but no one had heard of the missing Mrs Durand-Deacon. She then got on her bike and by ten o'clock was walking up the steps from Queen's Gate into the Onslow Court Hotel.

The hotel was decorated in fading art deco that had probably changed little from the 1920s when it was converted from five houses in a post-war hotel boom at the same time that other hotels like Claridges and The Cumberland were being built. Although a townhouse hotel not on the same scale, the Onslow Court provided a certain opulence for wealthy middle-class residents wishing to spend their retirement or widowhood in comfort.

Several ladies sat around the hallway and reception room after breakfast, enjoying a second cup of coffee brought to them by attentive waitresses and bell boys, and either reading the papers or sitting in quiet conversation. Sergeant Lambourne in her neat uniform could feel enquiring eyes watch her cross the hallway to the reception desk, wondering if she was bringing fresh news of the investigation or looking for clues or, in the language of the racier crime novels, casing the joint.

The fact was that the hotel could have hardly chosen a more prominent member of its clientele to disappear. Olive Durand-Deacon was intelligent, articulate, immaculately dressed and with an active record in her youth in the suffragette movement — it was rumoured that she'd lunched with Mrs Pankhurst — and a husband who had been a war hero. She was liked, always popping off to some show or concert in London, either alone or with one of her friends from the hotel. She had a sister who lived nearby in Kensington.

Although Olive was in her late sixties she looked like a woman in her fifties, while John Haigh on the table next to her was almost ageless in his Savile Row suits, silk ties and flashy cars. They made a handsome couple, and although they didn't socialise outside the hotel they were often seen chatting in the dining room or in the Tudor Room over a coffee or drink.

To allow her to get the lie of the land, Sergeant Lambourne had purposely not telephoned ahead of her visit. The atmosphere was very much as she expected: quiet, orderly, elderly even, with a reassuringly busy atmosphere that told you this was still a hotel and not a nursing home. It smelt fresh, there were flowers in the hall and on the reception desk, and every member of the staff she passed gave her a cheery smile and a polite good morning. She didn't want to admit it, but if one day she had to find somewhere on her own and had the money to do it then this might be the sort of place. Better win the pools first, though.

Her meeting with Mrs Robbie, the manageress, did nothing to change her views. She presented as more of the strong matronly type who might typically be in charge of a nursing home rather than the manageress of a hotel. Sergeant Lambourne told her she'd met Mrs Lane and Mr Haigh but wanted to know a little more about Mrs Durand-Deacon's life at the hotel.

'Well, from my point of view she is probably the perfect hotel guest,' said Mrs Robbie, determined to go on using the present tense even though her guest had now been missing three days. 'She always pays her bills on time, in person with a cheque at my office, is always there to help a fellow guest if anyone is in trouble or needs organising a bit, you know the sort of thing. Someone we rely on – this is why it's all the more surprising that she's disappeared like this without telling anyone where she's gone.'

'Would she tell you when she was going away?' asked Sergeant Lambourne.

'That's the thing: she's only stayed away once for any length of time in the five years she's been with us. Otherwise she's punctilious about telling us if she's going to miss a meal – dinner, for example, if she's going out to a concert or the theatre. This is what makes it all the more worrying.'

The two women sat looking at each other for a moment over Mrs Robbie's desk. 'Where does Mr Haigh fit in with all this, then?' asked Sergeant Lambourne, trying not to rush the question or make it sound too important.

Mrs Robbie looked out of her window at a taxi-driver trying to do a U-turn in Queen's Gate and getting hooted at by someone for his trouble. 'They are quite friendly. They sit on tables next to each other. They have some common interests like music and I believe there is some business project they have in mind. As I said, she always gives us notice that she'll miss a meal, which is more than I can say about Mr Haigh.'

'A bit young for one of your guests, if I may say so,' added Sergeant Lambourne.

'He used to have a bed-sitter up the road here in Queen's Gate Terrace with a friend but they got bombed out, and I think he likes someone looking after him these days. His friend used to come here to the hotel with him before Mr Haigh lived here permanently – Mac someone or other. They were as smart as each other, but his friend was a bit quiet. Haven't seen him for years, now I think about it.'

'When you say smart?'

'Like Mr Haigh, smart in a flashy sort of way. If it's not being rude, they both looked like they'd sell you a car or insurance before you knew it; you know what I mean, businessmen. Mr Haigh gets a barber up here from Victoria at two guineas a time for a shampoo and cut; if he's ordering a suit someone has to come up and fit it. He's a sort of 'money's no object' person, although you wouldn't always know it,' said Mrs Robbie, pursing her lips.

Sergeant Lambourne put down her notebook and looked Mrs Robbie in the eye. 'What do you mean?' she asked.

'Well, I have to say he can be one of our worst payers. Several times we've had to haul him up for getting behind with his bills. In fact, in the last couple of weeks I've had to threaten him with paying up or getting out. Not for the first time, as I said,' said Mrs Robbie, folding her arms across her not inconsiderable chest.

'And has he paid up?'

'I'm telling you this in confidence, of course, but he owed us nearly fifty pounds in the end, two months' rent, and then suddenly he ups and pays the whole lot in cash. I had to send Mrs Kirkwood, our head cashier, up to get it off him. It'll probably be alright now for a few months – it seems to go in cycles, when he is paid on his business deals, I expect. He's always out in the day on his rounds, but what he's rounding up none of us really know. I shouldn't talk about him like this, but he's a bit of a Flash Harry if you ask me. Harmless, though.'

They walked up together to Room 115 and Mrs Robbie, now getting used to going into Mrs Durand-Deacon's room to have a snoop for clues, showed the sergeant around almost as if it were her own room. She opened one of the wardrobe doors. 'You see, all her clothes are here. Her book only half read by her bed, and her suitcase on the wardrobe,' she said, peering inside the wardrobe as if even now she might spot something significant.

'What was she wearing on Friday?'

'Her Persian lamb coat. Always dressed beautifully, even to go down to Mr Haigh's factory.'

Sergeant Lambourne came back over the room to the wardrobe and Mrs Robbie. 'To go down where, did you say, Mrs Robbie?' she asked quietly.

'To Mr Haigh's factory in Crawley. He was going to drive her down only she didn't turn up to meet him, so he had to go on down alone. He didn't come back for dinner and didn't tell us, as usual.'

Mrs Robbie clicked her tongue in a demonstration as to what she had to put up with.

Sergeant Lambourne cycled back to the police station, where she found a criminal record sheet waiting on her desk for John George Haigh. A formidable list included obtaining money by false pretences, forging cheques and theft, attracting prison sentences of between fifteen months and four years.

Without reading the list for a second time, Sergeant Lambourne picked it up and marched off to Detective Inspector Symes's office.

Meanwhile John Haigh had woken up on that Monday morning with money on his mind, or rather the lack of it. The deadline for repaying the £50 loan to Edward Jones had passed on the previous Sunday evening and he didn't want to upset the old buffer. Edward was upset enough at the moment with his own customers not paying the bills and John didn't want to join the queue: after all, Edward had been pretty good about lending him money over the years and pushing him wasn't going to encourage loans when things got tight.

John went down for breakfast as usual in the hotel at eight. This time there was no need to say anything about the empty table next to him to either Mrs Lane or the waitresses. Everyone had taken to eating their meals in near silence now, keeping one eye on the dining-room door just in case Olive should make an appearance and say what a lovely time she'd had with her family and what was all the fuss about?

That reminded him: he'd better call in at Crawley on his rounds and see how she was cooking; with the police starting to sniff around he needed to get rid of the drum and its contents in the workshop. It should be a thinner soup by now, not a consommé perhaps but thin enough to throw out into the yard where it wouldn't be noticed with all the other junk and debris lying around there.

What he really missed was the drain that led straight into the river in his old London workshop in the Gloucester Road basement: now that was handy.

John then went up to his room to clean his teeth and give his hair a final brush with two silver-backed hairbrushes – each inscribed with his initials – a routine he followed every day, very often with a nail manicure and a moustache trim. He was meticulous about this and intolerant of anyone he considered unwashed or untidy. This was an attitude endorsed by Olive herself, and he was pleased that his last memory of her would be how beautifully she was dressed to come down to his factory, complete with fur coat, cloth hat and jewellery. The red handbag was typical; the last time she'd carried that was to a concert up the road at the Royal Albert Hall.

In the end John drove first to Crawley to check how things were going at the workshop. He poked the soup with the wooden stick and still found an obstinate lump of fat and piece of bone floating near the surface. For the second time he felt a little resentment towards Olive for carrying too much weight – still, too late for all that now as he started to scoop the liquid into a bucket and carry each load out into the yard to join the rest of the rubbish. A bucket full here or there hardly made any difference.

As the bucketfuls slowly reduced the level in the drum, John came to a halt with the sludge at the bottom, to include the lump of fat and bone sticking out accusingly at him. Like a cook trying to cover up a botched dish, he poured in a fresh quantity of acid and left it to work for another twenty-four hours. That should do it, he thought, and, wiping the stick on his apron, he replaced everything for the next day's inspection.

Next he was back in the car and off to Bull's the jewellers in Horsham, where they valued the rest of the jewellery at £130 on a supposedly probate basis. John mumbled something about his late aunt and said he'd come back if he decided to sell.

Last on his rounds, and with it looking likely now he was going to be able to get back to the hotel for lunch, he drove to Crawley to the West Street factory to put in an appearance and check no one was wanting to get into the workshop. But all was well, and with his rounds complete he drove to town, realising he suddenly had an appetite.

After lunch John was just starting to relax, listening to a couple of residents talking about a visit from a nice police lady in the morning and how she and Mrs Robbie had gone up to Olive's room for a good look round, when a couple of visitors arrived at reception asking if they might have a word with Mr Haigh. The receptionist knew John was taking his coffee in the Tudor Room and came in to tell him discreetly that a Mr Symes and another gentleman asked if they might have a word.

John went out into the hall, coffee cup and saucer still in hand, and was confronted by two police officers, looking for all purposes like Laurel and

Hardy. They introduced themselves as Inspectors Symes and Webb and asked if he would come into Mrs Robbie's office to help them with one or two questions.

Symes, the larger one who did most of the talking, asked John to sit down and confirmed he had no objection to John bringing in his coffee. 'We are making enquiries, Mr Haigh, with respect to a lady named Mrs Olive Durand-Deacon who is missing from this hotel,' he announced.

He had a squeaky voice, a centre parting and somewhat immobile face that now reminded John of a benign Billy Bunter.

John took a slow sip of this coffee. 'Yes, I thought you would see me, as I went with her friend Mrs Lane to the police station to report her missing. I will tell you all I know about it,' he said.

Symes took John's full names. 'Are you a married man, sir?' he asked.

'I am actually, but I haven't seen my wife for nearly fifteen years. The perfect marriage, really.'

Symes's face didn't move. Instead he wrote down John's answers, without the wisecracks, with a large fountain pen. 'I prefer Parkers myself,' said John, looking down at the pen.

'I'm sorry, sir?' said Symes.

'Your pen. I prefer Parker pens to Osmeroids,' replied John.

'I see, sir – well, everyone to his own, I suppose. And your occupation, please?'

'I'm an engineer and a director of Hurstlea Products Ltd of Crawley, Sussex, a firm of light engineers. I usually go down there once or twice a week. I am a patentee and have interests in various inventions,' replied John, taking another sip of his coffee, his small finger extended slightly from the handle of his cup.

'If we can turn to Mrs Durand-Deacon now, Mr Haigh. I understand you are helping her in some professional capacity in a scheme to manufacture false fingernails.'

'That's quite right, Inspector. She showed me some she had made of paper and had glued to her nails. She asked me if I could make something similar which could be sold. I suggested that she come down to the factory at Crawley to show us what she wanted. I arranged to take her down after lunch on Friday 18th, and I told my partner Mr Jones to expect me in the afternoon with the person who was interested in the fingernails. I got a bit delayed in the morning and Mrs Durand-Deacon said she wanted to go to the Army & Navy Stores to pick up some samples of existing types of artificial nails. We agreed she'd go on alone while I had lunch, and then she'd meet me at 2.30 outside the store. When I'd finished lunch I took the car down to meet her as arranged, but there was no sign of her. I waited an hour and then went on down to Crawley alone. That's about it, really,' said John, sitting back in his chair to allow the Inspector to catch up with his writing.

For a moment John had forgotten about Inspector Webb, who was sitting at the end of the desk, nodding quietly as John mapped out his afternoon that Friday with and without Mrs Durand-Deacon. 'Do you remember what she was wearing?' Webb asked with an encouraging smile.

John sat back up in his chair, as if he hadn't expected to be asked anything more. 'She was dressed in a black cloth hat and black astrakhan coat. She was carrying a small red plastic handbag, about nine inches by five. She was wearing a brass crucifix about five inches long on a chain around her neck,' said John, and when Symes had stopped writing both officers looked up, impressed that someone could remember such detail.

Symes broke the silence. 'I see, sir, and how did you spend the rest of the afternoon?'

'Well,' replied John, gaining in confidence and talking more quickly now. 'I got to Crawley at about twenty past four and attended to some business with some small fans we are making. I had my dinner in the Ancient Prior's Café in Crawley and left there just before seven and returned to the hotel at about eight o'clock. I went straight to my room.'

Webb at the end of the table was asking the next question before the last answer was written down. 'But didn't you make any enquiries as to why Mrs Durand-Deacon hadn't turned up and whether she was alright?'

'I can't remember now if I came down again that night,' said John, shrugging his shoulders.

'But surely, Mr Haigh,' persisted Webb, 'having made this appointment with Mrs Durand-Deacon you were curious as to what had happened to her, whether she was unwell or got delayed or whatever?'

'Well, I wasn't going to go up and bang on her door at that hour, was I?' replied John, showing the first signs of irritation. 'I do remember now coming down at about quarter to ten to see if Mrs Lane was in the Tudor Room, but she wasn't there.'

'Are you sure about that, sir?' Symes asked.

'She wasn't there – tucked up upstairs with all the other old birds, I expect.'

'No, I mean sure you came down to look for Mrs Lane?'

'Quite sure, Inspector. It'd been a long day and I went to bed then myself.'

John produced a packet of cigarettes, offered them round without any takers, and lit one up for himself.

Symes now put down his pen and folded his arms, as if whatever the answer to the next question he wasn't going to write it down. 'May I ask exactly what attracts you to this hotel, Mr Haigh? Most of these good ladies are of a certain age and retired, while you are a man in his middle age with a successful career.'

'That's easy to answer, Inspector. I had a bedsit here in Queen's Gate and so I know the area and my income fortunately allows me now to leave my bedsit days behind. Besides, I get on well with the old dears and look after them to a degree. Mrs Durand-Deacon is a good example, as a matter of fact. I regard the Onslow Court as my home rather than a hotel – we all do.' John stubbed out his cigarette in his saucer.

The officers thanked John for his time and co-operation and said they might want to talk to him further as the investigation continued. 'Feel free, gentlemen,' said John, shaking each by the hand. 'I'm not going anywhere.'

For a third morning John came down to breakfast beside an empty table. However, he could sense that the atmosphere in the dining room was changing: the conversation was returning to its usual buzz, there were fewer glances towards his corner and the dining-room door, and life generally was getting back to normal. But from John's side things were far from getting back to normal: there was a 40gal drum and its grisly contents to get rid of in Crawley and the small matter of repaying Edward Jones his money.

Otherwise things were moving in the right direction. He'd seen the police a couple of times and they couldn't lay anything on him. It was unfortunate that Mrs Lane knew that Olive was meant to be coming down to the factory, but he was pleased with the way he'd dealt with that with the story about the Army & Navy Stores. Disposal of the body was all but complete, and he'd got a reasonable quote for the jewellery, enough to keep Edward happy with a bit spare to give to the bank. All in all, it had been a good few days' work.

The batting order for his rounds was clear for the morning. First it was down to the Crawley workshop where he donned his rubber apron and poked around the contents of the drum with the wooden stick. There still seemed to be a lump of something at the bottom, but at least it was not bobbing around the surface and John decided that another twenty-four hours in fresh acid wasn't going to make any difference. Once again he dredged the drum with the bucket, throwing the contents out in the yard in the spot he'd used the previous day. Sure enough there were a couple of lumps at the bottom of the drum, but like all good soups you expected a bit of nourishment to lurk at the bottom and that could now go out with the rest.

Finally John half-carried, half-rolled the drum out into the yard and left it to look as unobtrusive as possible in the rest of the debris. The weather would do the rest of the job for him.

Next it was back in the car and a drive over to Horsham and Bull's the jewellers. Mr Gregg, an assistant in the shop, didn't need any reminding who John was when he appeared again with the jewellery. John unwrapped the jewellery from the duster he used for wiping the car windows and announced he'd decided to sell. Gregg quickly telephoned Mr Bull, the shop owner who'd made the valuation on the previous day to the man describing himself as Mr McLean of No. 32 St George's Drive, S.W.

'That's confirmed we would be interested in buying the jewellery,' Gregg said to John when he came back from the telephone. 'We can offer you one hundred pounds.'

'But you valued it at one hundred and thirty pounds yesterday,' John protested.

'That's right, sir, but that was for probate purposes. We now have to take the risk of selling the items at this price.'

'You'll get your price and more. My aunt was a wealthy woman, you know. She only bought the best.'

'I'm afraid that is what we have to offer.'

'Well, she'd be upset by this, but I'll have to take it,' said John.

Gregg then asked another assistant to fetch Mr McLean the money, but there was only £60 cash in the till, and so with the apologies for Mr Bull not being there to produce the balance, their customer accepted the cash and said he'd call the next day for the rest.

With this business done and £60 in his pocket, it was off to Crawley and the factory to repay Edward his loan. Well, part of the loan, anyway. As John drove over to Crawley he realised he had to be careful. If he gave Edward the full £50 and the remaining £10 to the bank to reduce his overdraft, then there was nothing left for himself.

'Sorry, Edward,' John announced breezily at the West Street office. 'The chap I was relying on let me down a bit. I can't repay it all this minute. What's the least you can take now?'

'I need at least thirty-six pounds to pay this insurance premium,' replied the long-suffering Jones, and watched his colleague count it out on the desk in £1 notes.

'You'll get the rest tomorrow,' promised John as his parting shot.

In the event, Edward Jones never got the rest of his money, and to rub salt into the wounds he received a visit that same afternoon from the Chelsea police wanting to know a lot more about the activities of his 'co-director' John George Haigh.

John drove back to London in a mood of near exultation. There was now no body for the police to find, he had repaid Edward at least part of the loan, and he still had £24 in his pocket to pay something back to the bank with a little bit over for himself. An enormous weight was lifted from his shoulders, and when he eventually turned into Queen's Gate to be confronted by a crowd of reporters waiting outside the hotel, John felt like a film star returning to his lair after a day's shooting. Yes, shooting, he liked the description.

He parked the Alvis conspicuously in front of the hotel, lingering a moment, cigarette in mouth, before he got out. When he did at last open the car door, there wasn't a member of the press unaware that the man they'd waited hours for in the cold had finally arrived. John pushed his way to the steps, grinning broadly and pretending to defend himself from the shoving and pushing going on around him. At first he muttered 'no comment' or 'nothing to say' out of the side of his mouth in the way he'd seen it in the newsreels but now, seeing himself plastered across the front page of every national newspaper in the morning, he turned modestly at the top of the steps to face his audience.

Most of the questions asked for news of Mrs Durand-Deacon. John looked somewhere over the heads of the reporters and said in clear tones, 'I have no further news on the whereabouts of my friend Mrs Olive Durand-Deacon. I am just as anxious as you or anyone else is on that score.'

'Are you close to Mrs Durand-Deacon?' someone else asked.

'As close as I am to you – we have tables next to each other in the dining room,' he replied, and his audience looked back up at him, unsure whether this was a joke. Whatever it was, it was good copy.

'We understand you and she had some business interests in common?'

'Mrs Durand-Deacon does not like painting her own nails, so she painted newspaper and stuck it on them. She knew I was one of those crazy inventors and she was very keen on the fingernails idea.'

'Was it going to make you a lot of money?'

'I am financially independent and could live without working at the factory.'

'When did you last see her, Mr Haigh?' came the next question.

'On Saturday – in fact I was the one who with another dear friend of hers reported her missing to the police,' said John, not wishing to waste another opportunity to point out he was the one who went to the police.

The next comment wiped the smile off John's face in the same way Mrs Lane's question about him taking Olive down to the factory had done at the weekend. 'I think you ought to know, Mr Haigh, that there are rumours that you have a criminal record,' came a voice from the back.

Then the smile was back again, and with a dismissive wave of the hand John said, 'Let's skip that – we are talking about Mrs Durand-Deacon. Now, are you gentlemen aware of her description with a photograph to put in your papers?'

Despite the confidence of the performance, there was a feeling among the gentlemen of the press, as they watched him conclude his impromptu press conference and walk back into the hotel in his smart coat and Savile Row suit, that they had just witnessed something akin to a public execution. In trying to act the cool, concerned friend of a missing person, the suspect had created exactly the opposite impression to hardened crime reporters who'd seen it all before: rather than a concerned friend, they were seeing another murderer who was about to be arrested.

On his way down to Horsham next morning to collect the rest of his jewellery money, John couldn't remember the name or address he'd given them at the shop. He'd given one to the jewellers in Putney when selling the watch, another to the Reigate cleaners for the coat, and now a third to Bull's. As he'd been there three times already he could be certain they'd recognise him.

In the event he needn't have worried because after entering the shop he walked into Mr Bull himself. 'Ah, Mr McLean,' he greeted John, 'you've come for your money. May I apologise, sir, for not having sufficient funds on the premises yesterday, but in my absence from the shop we have to limit the amount of cash on the premises.'

John shook him by the hand over the counter. 'Not to worry, Mr Bull. You can't be too careful these days.'

'Quite so, sir,' fussed Mr Bull. 'Now, for the same reason it's one of our house rules to check the address of our clients when it is a probate matter.'

John thought carefully for a moment. 'My aunt was in a nursing home in Guildford and I can't remember the address.'

'Not the deceased's address, sir, but your own,' effused Mr Bull.

'You'll have to remind me if I gave you my town or country address,' replied John.

Mr Bull opened a large sales ledger and ran his finger down the column. 'No. 32 St George's Drive, SW, Mr McLean. Is this a neighbourhood where one would find solicitors and legal gentlemen in general?' he asked.

'It is indeed, Mr Bull. You will recall we did some business two years ago when I brought in a cigarette case, gold watch and wedding ring, if

I remember correctly. I have a practice in Guildford and would be pleased to offer you some client probate shares at attractive prices if you are interested; however, it would have to be on the strict understanding that you mention this to no one. You see, it may not be strictly ethical if I am asking you to buy this jewellery on a similar basis.'

Mr Bull pondered this offer and assured him that he would consider it, but meanwhile he would not breathe a word. He handed John £40 in crisp £1 notes and bade him good morning.

John then drove to Crawley in time to present £5 to his bank to reduce his overdraft, which still stood at a formidable £78.

Finally a call at the West Street factory where John just wanted to make sure no one was making noises about the Leopold Road workshop. He found Edward in his office still looking as upset as he had all week. 'Hello, Edward, how's tricks?' he asked.

Edward looked up without enthusiasm and motioned him to sit down. 'I might ask you the same question, John. I've had the police round yesterday.'

John allowed himself to sit down before he replied. 'What are they snooping here for?' he asked.

'Again, I might ask you that. They seemed to want to know everything about you, short of whether you're a member of the Communist Party. This is all connected with the lady missing from your hotel, I take it?'

'Probably just checking everyone in the hotel. Did they know I had a record?'

'They did. I think they wondered if I wasn't implicated. They asked if I was aware my business partner had been in prison. When I said I was, they looked even more suspicious.'

'Sorry about that – I don't want to get you involved,' said John, drumming his fingers on the top of the desk.

'Look, John,' said Edward. 'I've known you a few years now and I know you have a chequered past. But if you're in any trouble I'd appreciate it if you kept well away from the factory. Times are hard enough without a scandal. I've helped you out with a loan, but that's about as much as I'm prepared to do, I'm afraid.'

John sat back in his seat and pushed his lower lip forward as if he were blowing a fly off the end of his nose. 'I suppose you haven't got a sandwich on the go, Edward?'

Edward smiled and opened his desk drawer for his wife's spam sandwiches.

'You're a good sort, Edward. If I had any sense I'd take a leaf out of your book and make an honest living,' said John, holding a sandwich in one hand and lighting a cigarette with the other. 'I can't seem to stop myself. I was selling some jewellery this morning, and when the old boy in the shop starting talking about probate, I suddenly went into that solicitor business, pretending I was selling probate shares on the cheap.'

'That got you four years last time. I won't ask where you got the jewellery this time.'

'Oh, I got that legit. But it was the solicitor business. You'd think I would have learnt by now. But you know I was making money hand over fist on that one. I couldn't cash the cheques quick enough. I only got caught because I couldn't bloody well spell Guildford on the notepaper.'

Edward was starting to relax. 'You're an idiot, John.'

'How much money do we make out of these inventions we scrap around with: metal buttons, toy soldiers and musical boxes? How much money do you make working your socks off here day and night eating spam sandwiches, while I lord it up there in town?'

Edward laughed again and shrugged his shoulders.

'I nearly got it right once. I went into partnership with a major in a dry-cleaning business. It was going well, money coming in. What happens – he's killed in a road accident and his wife wants to end the business. Well, that was it for me,' said John, helping himself to another sandwich.

'All I can say is that you've got the brains, John, so why not use them?' said Edward, screwing up the paper bag and throwing it into the bin.

'The thing is I do use them. I use them all the time. The HP car business needed brains to forge the documents. The Guildford business was the same: I had to find the shareholders, pretend I was a solicitor and sell them client shares at a knockdown price. I couldn't bank the cheques fast enough. I never thought about these schemes as right or wrong, just whether they'd make money. They always have. Our little inventions here come to nothing. Sorry, Edward, I know which I'd choose,' said John, getting to his feet to leave.

'There is one other thing, John,' said Edward. 'The keys to the workshop.'

'What about them?'

'I need them to shift some of those metal sheets back into store.'

John patted his coat pockets. 'I've left them in London. I'll drop them off next time. Even better, I'll take the sheets over for you.'

'What are you working on over there — it's been a while now?'

'Oh,' said John. 'It's just a conversion job. It's taken a bit longer than I thought but I'm nearly there.'

With that he was out of the door before Edward could say anything else.

12

If Edward Jones had any hopes that he and Hurstlea Products Ltd would avoid further involvement in the investigation, they were swiftly dashed two days later when the police returned to the West Street factory. This time the visit lasted seven hours and involved a full-scale search of the premises by Detective Sergeant Pat Heslin and other officers from Horsham Police Station. This followed a further police interview in London with John Haigh, who said little more than he had the last time.

During the search of a well-run factory making a variety of products, nothing more was being revealed to the police about either Haigh or Mrs Durand-Deacon.

'Where is Mr Haigh's office?' Heslin asked a harassed Edward.

'He doesn't have one as such. He has a desk upstairs, that's all. We work together on various projects on the bench downstairs, but that's about it.'

'But he's a director,' said Heslin.

'He's not a director, in fact, nor does he receive a salary from us. He's an unofficial representative, if you like. He's goes out there to customers to sell our products, and in return I let him use the premises for whatever project he's got going on. Lately it's been more of a case of him popping in to use the lavatory and then he's off again.'

'Did you discuss a project to make artificial fingernails with Mr Haigh?' asked Heslin.

'He did say to me the other day he had someone interested in making artificial fingernails, but it didn't sound commercial to me and I said I wasn't interested. He was going to bring whoever it was down to talk about it but they didn't turn up. I'm afraid I wasn't very sympathetic. I had too much going on here that week to worry about fingernails,' said Edward, aware that this week wasn't going much better either.

'But Mr Haigh must have somewhere he keeps his things,' persisted Heslin.

'Not here, Sergeant. He might keep something out at the workshop in Leopold Road. He's spending enough time out there at the moment,' said Edward.

Heslin sat up with ears pricked like a dog hearing something in the undergrowth. 'Leopold Road, Mr Jones, what's that?' he asked quietly.

'It's where we started the business. There's nothing much to it – one-up, one-down – we don't use it much now except for storing stuff like metal sheeting that we don't need over here. But John uses it as a workshop. In fact, he's got the keys while he does some conversion job.'

'Would he be over there now?' asked Heslin. 'I'd like to have a look around.'

'I doubt it. Anyway, I haven't the keys. He said he'd let me have them back when he was next down. I've got some stuff to go back over there.'

'I need to have a look, if you don't mind. Have you duplicate keys?'

'I have a spare of the mortice lock, but not the padlock.'

'I'd like to look now, without Mr Haigh knowing about it. We'll take care of the padlock.'

Edward looked up at the clock on his office wall. 'Not today, please. I've got a hell of a lot to do and most of the day has gone now. Tomorrow, perhaps. Do you work Saturdays?'

Heslin assured him they did and arranged to meet him at Giles Yard, Leopold Road, before lunch next morning.

When they met the next day Edward opened the mortice on the storeroom door with the spare key, but the padlock bracket was too small for the crowbar Heslin had brought. Instead he went over to debris on the far side of the yard and found a metal rod that soon did the trick.

Inside the storeroom the atmosphere was dark and damp, and even when Edward switched on the light the place felt too cold for work of any sort. Nevertheless, it was orderly if stark, with a rubber apron hanging on the far wall and a large square-shaped leather case embossed with an "H" on the lid on a nearby table. On the floor were three carboys packed with straw and a stirrup pump looking corroded and ill-used.

'What are those, Mr Jones?' asked Heslin, pointing to the carboys.

'They store acid and are being used by John on his project. I saw them at the end of last week when we were shifting some metal sheets over to

West Street. As I said, I don't use this place any longer and can't tell you much more,' said Edward.

'And the case – what would that hold?'

'Again, can't say. I haven't seen that before. It wasn't here when he were moving the sheets. You'll have to ask John.'

'I'd rather not for the moment,' replied Heslin. He tried to open the case but it was locked.

Not wanting to do a crowbar job on the case, nor remove it without a warrant, Heslin returned to the storeroom after lunch with Jones after a visit to Horsham Police Station to pick up a selection of skeleton keys. It didn't take long to open the case to find an assortment of papers and passports, bank books and ration cards, some in the name of Haigh, and others in unfamiliar names of McSwan and Henderson.

'Do you recognise the names, sir?' asked Heslin.

Jones shook his head.

Nor did he recognise the revolver in a holster tucked under all the papers, along with an envelope containing eight rounds of ammunition. Heslin took a delicate sniff at the end of the barrel, but all he could smell was gun oil.

Finally, tucked into one of the ration books, was a receipt from a firm of Reigate cleaners for a lady's Persian lamb coat.

Heslin had done his homework and remembered Haigh describing a black astrakhan coat. So what was he doing with a receipt for a Persian lamb coat? The revolver was not necessarily significant as it was one of many thousands of ex-service weapons in circulation after the war.

Nevertheless Heslin took the trouble to make his way home that afternoon via Reigate, only to find the cleaners shut on Saturday afternoons. He spent the evening tracking down the owners on the telephone, and on Sunday picked up the coat from the cleaners with Inspector Symes. The only thing that had made a member of staff suspicious at the time was that the customer did not seem the type to have a wife with such a valuable coat.

'Thing is, sir,' said Heslin to Symes, 'it's not a cape and it's not astrakhan.'

'If it was bloody bearskin I'd start to believe it was taken off the back of Mrs Durand-Deacon. The fact is that somebody sounding remarkably like our friend Mr Haigh has a coat that I bet you now turns out to be hers and he is thoughtfully getting it cleaned for her. So where is she and why can't she get it cleaned for herself?' asked Symes.

He just wanted something or someone else to turn up to point the finger conclusively at John Haigh and then, as he put it, they could all go home.

Someone else was also thinking about what Mrs Durand-Deacon might have been wearing the day she disappeared. Horace Bull, the jeweller, was at home reading his Sunday paper when an article on the front page started to raise the hair on the back of his neck. The piece ran photos of the missing lady from the London hotel along with a description of what she was wearing, including a list of her jewellery. The list sounded remarkably like the jewellery brought into the shop during the week by Mr McLean, and the photo of John Haigh giving his impromptu press conference on the steps of the Onslow Court Hotel was McLean alright. He'd check the jewellery first thing when he got into the shop tomorrow against the list, but he already knew he was right. His excitement was tempered by the fact that he appeared to have bought jewellery for £100 that had been stolen from this good lady, which would have to be returned to her, leaving him to find Mr McLean, or Haigh or whatever his name was, and ask for his money back.

Then again, he reflected, at least he hadn't bought any of those shares off the man.

13

On the Monday morning, after the telephone call from Mr Bull, Detective Inspector Symes went down to Horsham to identify the jewellery. They now had a gun, a Persian lamb coat that could match samples in Mrs Durand-Deacon's room at the hotel and the jewellery. Symes picked up the phone and spoke to DI Webb. 'Okay, Bert, wheel him in.'

Had Webb arrived at Onslow Court just a few seconds later, John Haigh might have earned himself a few more hours' freedom after the ten days he'd spent playing the innocent since Mrs Durand-Deacon disappeared. As the police car stopped outside the hotel, Webb saw him sitting in the Alvis, cigarette in the corner of his mouth, looking for something in the glovebox. Webb walked up to the car and John wound down his window. 'Good afternoon, Mr Haigh.'

'Good afternoon, Inspector, what can I do for you?'

'I'd like you to come down to the station to help us with a few more questions, please.'

'Of course,' replied John.

Inspector Webb was someone he'd got to know and rather liked after two lengthy meetings already at the hotel. For John there was no reason to suspect this was going to be any different to the others, and he got out of the car and beamed at him. 'I'll do anything to help, as you know,' he added.

At Chelsea Police Station, however, the atmosphere was rather less chummy. For a start they asked John to wait half an hour or so while, unknown to him, they checked Mrs Durand-Deacon's room in the hotel for a fur sample to match the coat. In fact the arrest had been so quick and easy anyway that no one had expected Webb to get back to the station so soon. John sat there without grumbling, smoking cigarettes and reading the paper, even dozing off occasionally.

'Sorry to keep you waiting, Mr Haigh,' said Symes, returning a little breathless from the hotel. 'But I've continued my enquiries into the disappearance of Mrs Durand-Deacon and there are some more questions.'

'Of course,' said John calmly.

'The first is whether you know anything about a Persian lamb coat we collected from a firm of dry cleaners in Reigate?'

'No, I don't think so. Should I?' replied John laconically.

'I'll come back to the coat, then. The other question is how many times have you been to Horsham?'

John reflected a moment. 'Well, I used to go to Horsham a lot, but lately I've only been there once, in the evening, to the pictures.'

Symes looked down at his notes, 'In fact you've been there in the morning recently on no less than four occasions, and I want you to tell me about that.'

John looked up at the wall behind Symes, the smile gone for a moment. 'I can see you know what you're talking about, and I will admit that the coat belonged to Mrs Durand-Deacon and that I sold her jewellery to Bull's the jewellers in Horsham, as you know.'

Without a further word DI Symes placed the parcel of jewellery on the desk and unwrapped the corners of the cloth for all to see the contents. Next he added the cleaner's ticket for the coat.

The smile slowly came back to John's lips. 'Yes, I wondered if you had got them when you started,' he said.

'I need to ask you how you came by this property, Mr Haigh, and where is Mrs Durand-Deacon? But first I have to caution you that you are not obliged to say anything unless you wish to do so but what you say may be given in evidence.'

'Yes, I know all that,' said John, starting to collect himself. 'It's a long story. Do you mind if I smoke?'

At this stage Symes wouldn't have minded if he'd wanted to stand on his head. John took a packet of cigarettes out of his pocket and offered them around. Finding no takers, he fumbled for his lighter and lit up, giving himself a few seconds to think. 'Well, it's one of blackmail, and I shall have to implicate many others. How do I stand about that?'

There was an inaudible groan around the room. 'What you have to say is entirely a matter for you,' replied Symes patiently, and seeing an urgent signal for him being made through the glass in the door, Symes left the room for ten minutes to deal with a couple of questions from forensics.

While he was out, John took a puff on his cigarette and turned to DI Webb. 'Tell me frankly, what are the chances of anyone being released from Broadmoor?'

Webb frowned. 'I'm afraid I can't discuss that sort of thing with you.'

'Well, if I told you the truth, you wouldn't believe me; it all sounds too fantastic.'

Rather than risk a further confession with the others still out of the room, Webb cautioned John again. 'Yes, yes, I know all that,' John repeated. 'I'll tell you all about it. Mrs Durand-Deacon no longer exists. She has disappeared completely and no trace of her can ever be found again.'

Webb looked as close to startled as he ever had in his long career. 'What do you mean? What's happened to her?'

'I mean I've destroyed her using acid. You will find the sludge which remains at Leopold Road. Every trace has gone. How can you prove murder when there's no body?' asked John, with a smile that said 'you're smart but not as smart as me'.

'I see,' said Webb, thinking that perhaps the question about Broadmoor wasn't so silly after all. 'Shall we wait for Inspector Symes to return – perhaps then you could explain?'

Symes was then urgently requested to come back into the interview room where Webb whispered in his ear what Haigh had said. 'I understand you've just said you destroyed Mrs Durand-Deacon by acid,' said Symes, managing to sound matter-of-fact.

'That is perfectly true, and it's a very long story and will take two hours to tell,' said John. 'May I take off my coat?'

The two officers followed suit and hung their jackets over the back of their chairs, sitting on the edge of their seats like children waiting to be read a story.

'I've been worried about the matter and fenced around about it in the vain hope that you lot might not find out about it,' John started.

The officers nodded sympathetically.

'Well,' John continued. 'The truth is that Mrs Durand-Deacon and I left the hotel together and went to Crawley together in my car. She was inveigled into going to Crawley by me in view of her interest in artificial fingernails.'

'This is the plan to manufacture fingernails at your premises that you've mentioned in previous statements,' said Symes.

'Yes, that's right. Having taken her into the storeroom at Leopold Road, I shot her in the back of the head while she was examining some cellophane for the fingernails project,' said John, pausing a moment to make sure they were all keeping up.

'This using the gun we found on the premises,' said Symes.

'That's right. Then I went out to the car and fetched in a drinking glass and made an incision, I think with a penknife, in the side of the throat, and collected a glass of blood, which I then drank,' he added, pausing again.

The expressions on the faces around the table were turning from shock to disbelief.

'Following that, I removed the coat she was wearing, a Persian lamb coat, and the jewellery, rings, necklace, earrings and crucifix, and put her in a forty-five gallon tank. I then filled the tank up with sulphuric acid, by means of a stirrup pump, from a carboy,' said John, continuing in an equally matter-of-fact way.

No one was asking questions any longer.

'I then left the acid to react. I should have said that in between having her in the tank and pumping in the acid, I went round to the Ancient Prior's for a cup of tea and an egg on toast. Talking of which, I could do with a cuppa now, if that's alright?' he asked, and Webb nodded to an officer to do the honours.

'Anyway, having left the tank to react, I brought the jewellery and revolver into the car and left the coat on the bench in the storeroom. I went to the George in Crawley for dinner and I remember it was late, about nine,' recalled John.

'I then came back to town and returned to the hotel about half past ten. That's about it, really,' he concluded, as the tea was brought in.

He took another cigarette out of its packet, this time without offering them around.

Symes pushed his notes aside for a moment and leaned towards John. 'You're not taking the Michael, old son, are you?' he asked.

'I'm sorry?' said John.

'You know, not taking the Mickey?'

'Absolutely not, Inspector. Sugar?' John asked, passing the bowl over the table.

14

The two police officers and John Haigh, no longer a suspect helping police with their enquiries but now a self-confessed murderer, sat back exhausted and allowed themselves a cigarette. While John remained composed, smiling as he moved from one grisly point to another, his inquisitors looked numbed, members of an audience where the script was moving out of their comfort zone.

Shelley Symes, who'd been doing most of the writing, collected the sheaves of paper and tried to put them in order. He was sweating profusely and his shirt was wet with perspiration. He looked at his watch and was surprised the statement had only taken an hour, although it felt like they'd been there all evening. 'Well, Mr Haigh,' he announced, 'I shall get this typed up and have you sign it. Before I do that there is a point I want to clear up. That's the question of the passport and ration books we found in the hat box in the names of McSwan and Henderson.'

John drained his cup of tea and stubbed out his cigarette in the saucer. He looked at his watch. 'That's another story,' he said cheerfully. 'I told you it would take two hours.'

Symes removed his cup and saucer from the top of his papers, opened his notebook again and picked up his pen. 'We've got the time,' he said.

'Well.' said John, 'This is covered briefly by the fact that in 1944 I disposed of Donald McSwan in the same way as Mrs Durand-Deacon.'

Symes hadn't written a word. 'You what?' he asked.

'I treated him the same way. He was less trouble than Mrs D-D because he wasn't overweight. She was a bit of a nuisance on that score, to be honest,' said John.

Symes put down his pen and took a hard look at John.

'I knew you wouldn't believe it,' said John, slapping his hands on his knees.

'Was this at Crawley as well?'

'No, no. This was in London, Gloucester Road. I had a basement there then. But there were others in Crawley as well.'

Symes turned to Webb. 'You'd better give us the full story, then,' said Webb.

Symes wrote down the time at the top of a new page. 'If you would start with their full names, please, and the address of, er,' Symes struggled to find the words, 'the venue of disposal.'

'I disposed of William Donald McSwan in the basement of 79 Gloucester Road, SW7, and his parents Donald McSwan and Amy McSwan in 1945 at the same address. In 1948, I disposed of Dr Archibald Henderson and his wife, Rosalie, in a similar manner at Leopold Road, Crawley,' recited John, word and date perfect.

Symes took a minute to finish writing. 'Well, shall we go through them in date order?'

'The son was called Donald but I can't remember his address. I remember the day I met him at The Goat, a pub in Kensington High Street, and after a few drinks we went to the basement in Gloucester Road that I was renting as a work room. I tapped him on the head with a sort of cosh I had, withdrew a glass of blood from his throat, as I did before, and drank it. He was dead in five minutes or so,' said John.

Donald McSwan, or 'Mac' as he was known, in fact was more than someone John had met in the pub. He had given John his first job as his chauffeur when John first came down to London. Mac ran a successful amusement arcade business, and John, with his talent for machines, helped with their repair and eventually helped Mac run the business as it expanded.

Mac was tall and handsome, with fair wavy hair and a moustache. He was vain and for some reason would never have his picture taken. He had friends of the opposite sex but never married or even became engaged. He dressed well and lived well, a life after John's heart, and they eventually took bedsit rooms in the same house in Queen's Gate Terrace, just up the road from the Onslow Court Hotel. When they were bombed out in 1944 Mac went back to live with his parents in Claverton Street, Pimlico, while John for the moment was left homeless, moving in for a time with Barbara Stephens's parents in Crawley.

However, there was murkier side to Donald McSwan. He had three convictions during the war for petty crimes, to include receiving lipsticks and unlawful possession of a US army torch, after being registered at the beginning of the war as a conscientious objector. He was directed to attend a medical board but failed to turn up and changed his address many times, presumably to stay ahead of the draft board. He had few friends and the only people who appeared to have any real interest in him were his parents, who also had very few friends.

One of these addresses for Mac was No. 22 Kempsford Gardens, London, SW5, owned by Walter Tatton-Edwards, where Mac lived for a few months from 10 May 1944 in a furnished room on the ground floor. In September that year he suddenly disappeared without giving any notice and leaving clothing such as shirts and pyjamas behind. Later someone claiming to be his father called and said his son had gone on business and would not be returning and that he had called to collect his son's belongings. Another tenant, Samuel Wagstaff, allowed this and Mac's clothing, typewriter and suitcase were taken away and the room was relet.

Tatton-Edwards and Wagstaff, landlord and tenant respectively at No. 22 Kempsford Gardens, both had criminal records but for more serious matters than Mac, including gross indecency and importuning male persons for immoral purposes. These men formed part of the London homosexual underworld, of which the tall, handsome and vain Donald McSwan was one. His only visitor at the house was a 16-year-old boy with fair hair, good-looking, well-spoken and well dressed. He called at least four times and was described by Mac as 'his nephew'. Wagstaff saw him with the boy in the West End on three or four occasions.

Another man who lived in and frequented the South Kensington scene – well-dressed like Donald McSwan and spending a lot of his time with him, good-looking, with a lot of charm, who said he had 'given up sex' in his early twenties after a brief unsuccessful marriage and who kept nocturnal and mysterious hours, rarely returning to his hotel before one in the morning, without explaining to anyone where he'd been – was John George Haigh.

'Then you disposed of McSwan in the same way?' Symes now asked John when he'd caught up with writing his notes.

'Well, sort of. I put him in a forty-gallon tank and disposed of him with acid, getting rid of the sludge down a manhole in the basement at Gloucester Road. I took his watch and other odds and ends, including an identity card, before I put him in the tank,' said John.

'How did you explain his disappearance to his family?' asked Webb.

'That wasn't too difficult, in fact. Remember it was the end of the war and men of Mac's age were still being called up. This didn't appeal much to Mac, and his parents knew he didn't like the idea, and so I just told them that he gone up to Scotland to disappear, as it were. They seemed to accept it, anyway. In fact I wrote a few letters as from Mac to his parents and posted them from Edinburgh and Glasgow, saying that he wanted to dispose of his various properties to me to look after while he was lying low. Quite simple, really,' said John, shrugging his shoulders.

'If the parents accepted their son's disappearance, then why did you have to get rid of them?' asked Webb.

'For the same reason I got rid of Mac. I needed the money, and they had a few properties between them. I took them separately to the basement and disposed of them in the same way as Mac. Their files are in my hotel room and they'll give you all the details of the properties I made over to myself after they were dead – you'll find it all there, and some more ration books I got by producing their identity cards. I never went short, and I was able to look after one or two of the old girls in the hotel,' said John, smiling as he remembered the little extras he could bring everyone at Onslow Court.

Symes and Webb, who'd both visited Haigh first in the hotel, could see him now seated in the Tudor Room, passing over some titbits from Harrods or Fortnum and Mason to fellow residents to take up to their rooms.

The clothing coupons he would use for himself, as a man who always liked to look his best.

'And the Hendersons?' asked Symes.

'The same,' replied John.

'Exactly the same?'

'Well, not exactly the same. I dealt with them at Crawley rather than Gloucester Road.'

Symes considered starting a new page in his notebook and then thought he'd used enough paper already. He was tempted to write 'Hendersons – the same' and save even more paper, but told himself not get hysterical.

'Perhaps you could tell us who the Hendersons were and how you met them?' Symes asked.

'Certainly, anything to help,' said John, returning to old bonhomie. 'I met them by answering an advertisement offering their property at 22 Ladbroke Square for sale. I got to know them a bit during the negotiations and we became friends. In the end I didn't buy it – to be honest I couldn't have afforded it anyway – and they sold it elsewhere and moved to 16 Dawes Road, Fulham.'

In fact Rose Henderson had written to her brother Arnold Burlin, 'of the scores of stupid people I've met I've just been introduced to the stupidest of them all. I offered him 22, Ladbroke Square lock, stock and barrel for £8,750 and he said "That's too cheap, but if you will accept £10,500 it's a deal".' Burlin's response had been 'When you meet a man who talks like that you should run for your life.'

Dr Archie Henderson had run a successful West End practice until drink forced him to quit. Left with considerable wealth after the death of his first wife, who left him £20,000, life lurched from one alcoholic venture to another, with him and Rose owning and running a toyshop called The Doll's Hospital in Fulham Road, and then having an interest in a typical Haigh project of making rocking horses out of tubular steel.

John Haigh became a magnet to people with half-formed, half-baked manufacturing ideas, especially if they had the money to pay for them. When he was drunk Henderson was a violent tartar, to use the description of one of his employees, but generous and good-natured when sober. Rose was his second wife, eight years younger, glamorous and long-suffering, and there were terrible quarrels between them, sometimes ending with Rose screaming for help in the house. Often Archie would be away from the house for long periods during the day, returning late at night after the household staff had gone to bed. This followed a similar cycle with John Haigh, who would often not return to his hotel before one in the morning.

'When are we talking about?' asked Symes, referring to John's friendship with the Hendersons.

'This was between November 1947 and February 1948. In February 1948 they were staying at the Hotel Metropole, Brighton, and on a pretext I needn't go into here I took Dr Henderson to Crawley and disposed of him in the storeroom at Leopold Road by shooting him in the head with his own revolver, which I had taken from his house in Fulham.'

Symes paused there a moment to catch up. 'Is this the same revolver you used for Mrs Durand-Deacon?' he asked.

'Yes, that's right. He never used it – never noticed it had gone.'

'Anyway,' continued Symes, 'why did you use the Crawley storeroom this time?'

'Only because I'd given up the tenancy on Gloucester Road after being given the use of the storeroom by Edward Jones. Less convenient really because Gloucester Road had a proper drain in the floor, while with the Crawley storeroom I had to chuck everything out into the yard.'

'So we won't find anything of Dr Henderson in the yard now?'

'Just a bit of sludge – oh, and possibly a left foot. I had a bit of trouble with him, like Mrs Durand-Deacon.'

'A left foot,' articulated Symes making his note.

'I think it was the left.'

'But a foot, anyway.'

'As I said, Gloucester Road was better because there was a proper drain there and if anything remained it was washed straight down into the river.

Anyway, no use moaning about it now. I think Mrs Durand-Deacon's handbag is out there in the yard as well because it wouldn't dissolve – plastic, I suppose.'

'And Mrs Henderson?' asked Symes, deciding this time to start a new page.

'The same, except I had to invent a reason to bring her up to Crawley on the same day. I went down to Brighton and said her husband was very ill and that she needed to come to Crawley. I said he'd had a heart attack and that things were looking bad. I took her back up to Crawley myself in the car, shot her in the storeroom and put her in a drum of acid,' said John.

'So that was two of them in separate drums?'

'They took about the same time to dissolve, about forty-eight hours or so.'

'Except for Dr Henderson's left foot,' said Symes quietly.

'I should have added that I took a glass of blood from each of them, as I did with each of the McSwans.'

'In the same manner?'

'Using a penknife with an incision in the throat – for all four of them.'

Symes finished his note and sat silent or a moment. 'I think I need a glass of water,' he said. 'Anyone else want something?'

'I could murder a cup of tea,' said John.

'Make a change, I suppose,' said Symes dryly, and everyone allowed themselves a smile in what had been a grim two hours.

When the duty sergeant had brought in teas, glasses of water and a plate of biscuits they'd confiscated in a black market food raid, everyone settled for what they hoped was the last lap of the story.

'Did you also dispose of the Hendersons' property in the way you did the others?' asked Symes, perspiring freely again and wanting to bring it all to an end.

'Yes, that's right. I removed Dr Henderson's gold cigarette case, his gold pocket watch and chain, and from Mrs Henderson her wedding ring and diamond ring, and sold all these at Bull's the jewellers in Horsham for about three hundred pounds.'

'Mr Bull hasn't done badly out of you, then?'

'No, but he wasn't aware of where this was all coming from, of course.'

'A lot of deaths in the family if it was probate?'

'Well, no, I said it was probate and I was acting for various clients in some legal capacity.'

Inspector Webb asked how the Hendersons' sudden disappearance from the hotel had been explained without raising suspicion, not least because they hadn't paid their hotel bill. 'I paid their bill at the Metropole,' John explained. 'I collected their luggage and their red setter dog and took the luggage up to Dawes Road in Fulham. I made some excuse about them being called away – but all the hotel was worried about was the bill being paid and their room cleared, including the dog. In fact they were very grateful to me for taking the trouble to come down and explain what was happening. I couldn't have left Pat, though.'

'Pat?' asked Webb.

'Their dog – I kept him at the Onslow Court for a bit, until I had to send him to kennels in the country because of his night blindness.'

'Did he recover?' asked Webb, hoping for at least one happy ending.

'No, he went completely blind unfortunately.'

'Finally, then, how did you explain to their family and friends that this couple had suddenly vanished, disappeared into thin air?'

'I kept the family quiet by writing letters to Mrs Henderson's brother, Arnold Burlin, in Manchester, saying they had gone to South Africa. He was becoming suspicious and was threatening to go to the police. I might have had to deal with him if things had continued.'

Burlin had come very near to reporting his sister's disappearance after a SOS had been put out by the BBC asking Rose to visit her dying mother in Manchester. John had said to Burlin that before he reported to the police 'you should come and see me'. Burlin had seen a photo in the Sunday papers of Mrs Durand-Deacon and immediately rang the police; on the woman's finger was a ring, a blue sapphire with a diamond on either side. It looked exactly like his sister's engagement ring.

Symes put down his pen and surveyed the scene. Here they were, for all purposes looking as if they'd finished a convivial tea party, swapping stories of abduction and murder, acid baths and body parts, stripping bodies of their jewellery and converting their assets and properties. And there was the certainty that, if their guest had not been caught, he would have gone on doing more of the same to fund London hotels, fast cars and nights at the opera, with his only overheads as running a damp workroom – although that was free as long as he acted as a rep for Hurstlea – three carboys of sulphuric acid, a few non-corrosive oil drums, a stolen revolver and two sheets of red cellophane.

And yet all through this tale of horror and deceit – and Symes could bet he spoke for nearly everyone who'd come into contact with him, including his victims – it was impossible not to like John George Haigh, with his infectious smile, his courtesy and impeccable manners.

16

Next day, Tuesday 1 March, Chief Inspector Guy Mahon, a senior member of Scotland Yard's flying squad and now in general command of the investigation, accompanied by Dr Keith Simpson, an eminent pathologist from Guy's Hospital, travelled down to Crawley. They were on a forensic mission to pick up as many bits and pieces as they could from the workroom that would be needed as exhibits for a trial and to see exactly what was in the yard outside the workroom.

Despite his years as a detective, and with a long career behind him, walking into a room where he knew a woman had been shot in cold blood gave Guy Mahon the shivers. Even in daytime the place was badly lit, with a bare bulb hanging from the ceiling over a workbench running under the front windows and along the far side of the room. The three acid carboys still sat on the floor, along with a bucket and a wooden rod whose end looked as if it had been chewed by a dog.

On the workbench in front of one the windows were two pieces of red cellophane, a roll of cotton wool and a gas mask case. Mahon bent over to scrutinise the pieces of cellophane on the bench, very much as Mrs Durand-Deacon must have done in her last seconds, and as he did so noticed a cloud of tiny red specks on the whitewashed wall in front of him. 'We'll have those for a start,' he said to Dr Simpson.

To the right of the door was a permanent ladder fixed to the wall leading up to the loft. Mahon thought he ought to have a look, but there was nothing up there apart from some old pieces of lumber and coils of wire.

As he climbed back downstairs, he wondered how anyone kept warm enough in winter to actually work at the bench, where presumably Haigh had spent hours fiddling around with his inventions. 'What a bloody awful place to get shot in,' he said to Dr Simpson. 'Come on, let's have a look around outside.'

Outside in the yard the scene was hardly any less bleak, but it was the far side that interested Mahon and Simpson most. If anyone was going to tip anything out that he didn't want noticed, it would be here among the discarded sheets of metal, piping and old oil drums, all the rubbish and detritus collected over the years by a small engineering firm.

Mahon started by separating three oil drums: one green and looking the more recently used, the others rusting and starting to decompose. After a thorough combing of the other items, to reveal a stained but otherwise recognisable pink handbag, some bone and a lump of fat that Dr Simpson said he wanted to examine, Mahon ordered that the topsoil be dug up to a depth of 3in and put into boxes for a thorough sifting by Dr Simpson.

Meanwhile back in London DI Symes made a further visit to Room 404 in the Onslow Court Hotel. As a contrast to his Crawley workroom, John Haigh's hotel room on the fourth floor was warm, comfortably furnished with a wardrobe, chest of drawers and a large desk, and was tidy. It looked out of the front of the building, high above the bustle of Queen's Gate, and the two sash windows made it a bright and cheerful room. There was an impressive array of shirts and suits in the wardrobe, rows of shoes fitted with cedar trees, and a collection of theatre and concert programmes on the shelves above his desk.

Symes was sifting through the contents of the desk, which included files of papers and documents relating to the McSwans and Hendersons, when he noticed what looked like a scribbled shopping list sitting on top of the desk. The list included a drum, with enamelling and a brush, H_2SO_4 (sulphuric acid), a stirrup pump, gloves, apron, rags, a cotton wool pad and finally some red paper. Added were various addresses where one might buy oil drums with respective sizes.

Down one side of the list had been scribbled 'LAUNDRY' in capital letters and then crossed out, presumably when the laundry had been sent.

Symes could almost see John Haigh now, walking through the door, weary after a long day on the road and, on seeing the list, say, 'Ah, I was looking for that. I thought I'd left it in the car. Thank you so much.'

The Alvis was the last item of John Haigh's property to be searched by the police. Mahon had promised himself the car, and he chose to drive it down personally from where it sat in front of the hotel to the yard at the back of Chelsea Police Station. Even on his pay as a chief inspector, he couldn't afford anything like an Alvis, beautifully finished in maroon with walnut fascia and leather upholstery. He imagined what was going through Haigh's mind as he drove Mrs Durand-Deacon down to Crawley on that Friday afternoon, chatting amiably to her about making fingernails and how long it might all take and how much money she was going to make, while all the time he knew exactly what he was going to do with her the minute they walked through the door of that miserable little workshop of his.

Having reached Chelsea and parked up at the back of the station, Mahon had a good look through the boot, under the seats and finally in the glovebox, where he found a penknife with its blades still open, showing traces of dried blood.

Mahon carefully took his handkerchief out of his pocket and laid the knife on it, folding the corners into a neat parcel to prevent any contamination. After the fantastic stories from Haigh in his last interview about drinking the blood of his victim after making an incision in her throat, perhaps the story was true after all. But if it was true, where was the glass? There was nothing in the workshop, nothing to even make a cup of tea.

Finally Mahon covered the Alvis in 'Do Not Touch' sheeting, and as he did so a car carrying John Haigh in the back seat passed through the yard on its way to Horsham Police Station. John caught a final glimpse of his pride and joy, the car he loved to be seen in, now looking so sorry for itself wrapped in paper like a body in a shroud. For the first time he felt a twinge of regret for the life he was leaving behind, not for the victims and the six lives he'd cut short but for his cars, the hotel, the Saturday afternoons with Barbara, for Hurstlea and the days playing with his inventions in the Crawley workshop.

But this soon passed as he struck up conversation with his escort on the way down to Horsham. He was ushered into the charging room where he was confronted by Detective Superintendent Percy Eagle, Head of Sussex CID. There was a moment or two while a charge sheet was completed.

Finally at 2.15 p.m. he was asked to stand. DS Eagle cleared his throat. 'John George Haigh,' he intoned, 'I charge you with the murder of Mrs Olive Durand-Deacon on the eighteenth of February of this year at Crawley.'

He cautioned the prisoner, who was then asked if he had anything to say.

John looked quizzically back at DS Eagle and flatly replied, 'I have nothing to say.'

17

Without further ado, John was whisked back into the car and taken over to the Magistrates Court in Market Square, Horsham. Preparations were made to clear the building to allow him to be brought into a side entrance and dealt with as quickly as possible. Word had got around town, and there was a crowd of onlookers and press surging around the steps as he was escorted by two police officers from the car to the door. John, smiling to his audience like some film star, was dressed immaculately, washed and shaven, with his hair brushed back and shining.

The two magistrates taking the hearing came face to face with the prisoner in the dock as the court was asked to rise. The clerk to the court read out the charge. Superintendent Eagle, who was today the sole representative for the prosecution, stepped into the witness box to give a cursory description of his visit to Leopold Road without a mention of blood, guts or body parts. John, as yet unrepresented by a solicitor, was then told by the clerk to stand and asked if he wanted to say anything to the superintendent. He shook his head and smiled confidently back at the clerk.

The only other question to be cleared up was whether John should be given legal aid or indeed whether he was applying for it. It was going through his mind that if he accepted legal aid to be represented by a solicitor and barrister at the taxpayer's expense, it might restrict the possibility of selling his story to the press. Looking at the reception outside, it was obvious he was not going to have much trouble in naming his price or at least having a newspaper pay for his defence team in return for his story. It was something he'd always dreamt about as he progressed from petty fraud to the more serious business of impersonating solicitors and receiving a little more celebrity. A top team of barristers would give him more chance of getting into Broadmoor, where he saw himself continuing to write his story and even a book; perhaps he would also make a film one day, with him playing the leading part.

Meanwhile, what to say to the court? John didn't want to tarnish the image of the man of means, with the posh London address and the Savile Row suit. He couldn't quite bring himself to say he was broke and would need the state to pay for his defence. 'Could we deal with legal aid next time?' he asked in a businesslike manner. 'That'll give me the time to arrange things.'

The magistrates nodded and remanded him to be held at Lewes prison until 11 March.

The whole hearing had taken barely quarter of an hour, hardly time for John to consider what the police were saying to the court in their brief submission and then what to do about legal aid, let alone any chance to scan the public gallery for the person to whom this was making the least sense. This was Barbara's first time in court and the whole point of the proceedings was lost on her, whether they were sending him to a larger court, whether he was to plead guilty or not guilty, whether there would be a jury and whether the whole thing wasn't some ghastly mistake.

It was only a week ago that the two of them were having tea at the Onslow Court Hotel, rather enjoying the drama of the missing Mrs Durand-Deacon. John had seemed at his most relaxed and witty, pointing out the diminutive Mrs Lane and how he'd take her on Sunday to report the disappearance to the Chelsea police.

The only solution to this nightmare must be that the police were desperate after a week to arrest somebody over the Disappearing Durand-Deacon, as John called her, and he, as one of the few men in the place, was a good target. Anyone in court that day could see how ludicrous the idea was; she should know as she'd been his companion for the last five years, during which they'd written to one another once or twice a week and met every weekend in what she'd always regarded as a loving relationship. The idea that he had been murdering people was grotesque.

But Barbara was not someone who gave in easily, and she followed the police car carrying John to Lewes with the demand that she be allowed to see him and sort the thing out. The prison staff were formal but kindly to the innocent young girl, who they probably imagined had been duped by an older man who looked and acted like an Italian mobster. She looked a nice kid who'd got her pretty fingers burnt meddling with a man twice her age. They'd seen it all before. They suggested she come back next morning, and as he was on remand there seemed no reason why she shouldn't visit him, provided he agreed of course.

Dear God, provided he agreed. All that she could think of was that he must be going insane with all this and desperate to see her with some instructions on how she could help. She'd hoped he'd look over to her in the public gallery at court to reassure her but everything there happened so quickly.

The next morning she was back at the prison at the appointed time and was ushered into a visitors' room, to a booth with dividing glass to prevent anything more intimate than talking.

As she walked into the world of washed floors and disinfectant in Lewes prison, half of her expected to find John already discharged and even waiting for her in the Alvis, all smiles and forgiving and saying wasn't it all fun. Instead he was brought into the visitors' room, still smiling but wearing his shirt open at the neck with his suit trousers. She'd never seen him without a tie before.

He was seated opposite her on the other side of the glass. 'Baba, how sweet of you to come,' he was barely audible through the speech holes in the glass.

'How are you, darling?' was all she could think of asking.

'Well, not too bad. They've put me up in the medical wing because I'm not a youth offender like the others here, but I told them I took that as an insult,' said John, laughing at his own joke.

Barbara looked at him, as content and at ease as he might have been if she was meeting him for tea at the hotel. There was no protest, no criticism of the police or the prison, no desperate requests for a solicitor or to get him out of there. Nothing was missing except the jacket and tie.

'Sorry I can't offer you tea,' said John, as if he were reading her mind. 'Actually the tea isn't bad, but no scones,' he added, looking over to the prison officer keeping an eye on them.

Barbara's face contorted and the tears started to roll down her cheeks. She leaned closer to the glass and poked a couple of fingers through the holes: the nearest she could get to grabbing and shaking him.

'Tell me it's all a terrible mistake, John, please.'

John didn't like seeing people upset, especially Barbara. She didn't have to be a lip-reader to decipher his reply. 'I'm sorry,' he whispered.

It took a few seconds for this to sink in, and then the tears really started. 'Then why didn't you murder me? You had the chances, didn't you?' she screamed.

The warder took a step towards them but John motioned to him that it was alright. 'Now don't be silly, Ba.'

'Why not then?'

'Because that was not the way it was. The others were different and you were nothing to do with it.'

'But why, for God's sake?'

'Well, not for the money. I drank their blood.'

Barbara wiped away her tears and collected herself. 'Oh for God's sake, John, stop acting mad. Tell me this is all a bad dream and how you're going to get yourself out of it.'

John put his fingers up to touch hers at the grille. He leaned forward in his seat. 'They'll put me somewhere where they can keep an eye on me. Broadmoor I expect – I'll be out in six years, just you see,' he said.

'Are you sure?' asked Barbara, wiping her eyes. 'Where is Broadmoor – is it nice?'

'You could drive it in an hour. You can come and see me on Saturdays like you do at the Onslow.'

Barbara visibly relaxed a little. 'The papers are calling you a vampire, it's quite ridiculous.'

'I'll sue them. It's a stain on my character,' said John, laughing again at his little joke.

'Be serious, darling, please. I shall be hopeless without you.'

'How are the parents taking it?'

'Badly. They don't know what's going on either. There are pressmen outside the house. Mum gives them cups of tea and says you're an angel.'

They looked at each other, unsure what to say next.

The officer took the opportunity to look at his watch. 'Five minutes, ladies and gentlemen, please,' he chanted like a publican, trying to make it less painful for a couple he could see struggling.

'Is there anything you want, darling?' asked Barbara.

'No,' replied John when the warder came over to escort him back to the cells. 'But there's a dog in a dog's home in Horsham I send money to for looking after him. I can't remember the name of the place. But can you make sure they get paid.'

'A dog?'

'His name's Pat. He's a red setter, but he's blind. He used to belong to friends of mine.'

Barbara watched the man she was to marry one day being led away to his cell. Later, perhaps, he'd be taken to somewhere called Broadmoor, although the papers were predicting something far worse that she couldn't begin to think about.

Before John had even reached the door of the visitors' room he was already chatting to his escort and making him laugh.

18

The next day, Friday 4 March, was a busy day for John Haigh, in a cell he shared with a young offender who woke him by shouting through the cell door window for his medication. But it wasn't clear whether anyone was listening to him or indeed very interested in him or his medication. While all this was going on, John allowed himself ten minutes in his bunk to map out his day: there was a further statement to make to Inspector Webb who was coming down to see him from Chelsea, a telegram to answer from the *News of the World* asking to meet to discuss 'an interesting proposal' and a letter to write to Barbara.

His day started with a follow-up letter from the *News of the World* to yesterday's telegram:

```
                                      News of the World
                                  30, Bouverie Street,
                                     Fleet Street EC4
                                             2.3.49
Dear Mr Haigh,
   It has been reported that you stated in Court yesterday
that you wished to apply for legal aid, and that you told
the Chairman of the magistrates that you had not sufficient
means for this purpose.
   The News of the World is prepared to place the best legal
aid at your disposal, and if you wish to avail yourself of
this offer our solicitors will see you immediately.
```

> Alternatively, if you wish to instruct solicitors of your own choice, we will get in touch with them for you and make all necessary financial arrangements.
>
> Please state what your wishes are and they will be communicated to us.
>
> Yours faithfully,
>
> S.W. Somerfield for the Editor

John by now regarded Inspector Bert Webb as a confidant and friend among all the police officers he'd met so far and it was the question of legal representation that started their conversation today. Webb was the one he'd asked about the chances of getting out of Broadmoor, and this time John specifically asked for him to come down from London. For his part Webb didn't need asking twice, but short of John suddenly denying everything he couldn't think what he was going to come up with this time.

Their meeting today was conducted in rather more civilised circumstances than the earlier meeting with Barbara, in a proper interview room with a table and chairs where John would be alone with the inspector. Webb was already waiting for him as he came into the room and stood to shake his hand and motion him to the chair on the other side of the desk. 'Hello John, how are you doing?' he asked cheerily.

'Not bad at all, thank you, Inspector,' came the equally cheerful reply.

One point had troubled Webb through the first hearing and he brought it up now. 'Have you got yourself a solicitor yet, John?' he asked.

'Well, funny you should say that because I'm probably getting that sorted out today. I got a letter from a chap at the *News of the World* offering me legal aid.'

'You need someone really if you're giving us these statements,' said Webb, not wanting to sound too keen on the idea in case he was sent back to London empty-handed. 'Barbara alright?'

'Bit upset, you know.'

'Not surprising, I suppose. Anyway, John, what can I do for you today?'

Webb was using a Christian name, but he was alone with his suspect now and wanted things to be informal, especially if this was only about John's car or something he wanted brought down from his hotel room.

'Well,' said John, looking over to the frosted glass in the door to check no one was listening. 'Before you caution me, can I ask you something, off the record?'

'You can try, I suppose.'

'You know I asked you what my chances were of getting out of Broadmoor. Well, what do you think my chances are of getting *into* Broadmoor?'

Webb put down his pencil. He wasn't going to record any of this this time. 'I'm afraid my answer's the same: that's up to you and why you need a solicitor. But I've sat through a couple of murder trials where insanity was the defence and the only doctor I remember is a Dr Yellowlees. He seemed to know what he was talking about.'

'Yellowknees,' mused John. 'Not much of a name.'

'Yellowlees – some egghead psycho from Harley Street. Do you really want to go to Broadmoor, John? You'll meet some real nutters there.'

'Better than the alternative,' said John.

Webb gave a grim nod. 'You wanted to see me about something else, I imagine,' he said after cautioning him.

'That's right. I wanted to check that the statement I gave you on Monday all adds up. I mean, are you satisfied with it?'

'As far as we know it all adds up.'

'You see, you can check up on the McSwans, Hendersons and Mrs Durand-Deacon but there are others I mentioned on Monday that aren't going to be so easy.'

'Is that because you can't remember who they are or where you disposed of them?'

'It's because I didn't really know them very well and it would be hard to trace them after all this time.'

'Well, we can try,' said Webb, picking up his pencil. 'Do want to give me their names?'

'The first was about a couple of months after Mac. She was a woman about 33 years old.'

'Do you know her name?'

John shook his head. 'She was five feet seven inches tall, slim dark hair. I'd never met her before.'

'Where did you meet her?'

'In Hammersmith, somewhere between the Broadway and Hammersmith Bridge. We chatted for bit, about twenty minutes. Then I asked her if she'd walk back to Kensington with me. We took the tube to Gloucester Road and I invited her into what I called my flat – the basement at number 79. I hit her over the head with a cosh and as usual tapped her for a drink of blood.'

Webb was almost getting used to writing down the grim details. 'Is that all?' he asked.

'That's about it for her. There was nothing much in her handbag – I remember it because it was a sort of dark envelope-type bag – and disposed of the body in the same way I did all the others.'

'Anyone else?'

'A youngish chap, in the autumn of the same year.'

'Any name?'

'No name that I can remember. I met him in the Goat in Kensington High Street. He was about 35 and wearing a blue double-breasted suit. I'd seen him before there and I had a drink and a snack with him and we talked about pin-tables. I asked him to come down to what I described this time as my workshop in Gloucester Road, and the same thing happened as before.'

'Take anything off him?' asked Webb.

'Not really, he had no jewellery and no more than a quid or so in his pocket.'

'Is that it, then?' asked Webb, trying not to tell himself John was making it up. They all seemed conveniently anonymous and not the way John had worked before.

'One more,' said John. 'Between late summer and early autumn last year in Eastbourne. I met a girl on the front near the Mansion Hotel, about 8 p.m.'

'Any name this time?'

'Mary, she said. She was shorter than me, black hair, not English – Welsh probably. She was wearing a white and green summer dress, white beach shoes and a light-coloured handbag.'

'You remember all this very well.'

'Well, you do, don't you, when you have to get rid of all the stuff,' said John, screwing up his eyes trying to remember the scene. 'We went to Hastings and had a meal at a café on the front in the old part of town. I took her back to Leopold Road in the car, hit her with the cosh and tapped her for blood. I used one of the tubs I used for the Hendersons to get rid of the body, that's why the tubs you've found in the yard are in bad condition.'

'Did she have any property?'

'Nothing except a bottle of scent that I kept and which Inspector Mahon asked me about the other day.'

Webb finished his note and put down his pencil. One of the prison staff poked his head around the door. 'Cup of tea, Inspector?'

'Yes, please – and one for our friend here. He's been telling me how well you're looking after him.'

The young officer looked pleased. 'Afraid we've had to put him up in the hospital wing because we're mainly young offenders here.'

Webb used the tea as a break. 'Do you want any clothes brought down from your room?'

'Couple of suits and shirts would be handy, and underclothes. Didn't get a chance to pack,' said John. 'Very grateful to you.'

For the first time John Haigh, self-confessed serial killer and vampire, looked the vulnerable choirboy he was when he started life, stirring his tea with the serious concentration he might have used in a break in choir practice. 'Very grateful. Sorry to have caused you all this trouble. If I get through all this you'll have to come up to tea at the hotel. They do a very nice cream tea at the Onslow. Barbara always likes tea there – she'll miss that.'

Webb picked up his pencil. 'Any more?' he asked.

John drained his cup and put it carefully back on to the saucer. 'No, that's it. No one else. That's enough, do you think?'

'Nothing else you want to tell me?'

John shook his head and pushed the empty cup and saucer back over the table. 'Nothing, Inspector, except that was a very nice cup of tea.'

John Haigh's next visitor arrived after lunch and was already ensconced in an interview room, drinking a cup of tea and smoking a cigarette, when John was taken to meet him. His Burberry coat was slung over the back of the chair and his trilby hat thrown carelessly on the desk. As he was in an interview rather than visitors' room, John assumed he was police or something to do with the law.

'Nice place you've got here,' he greeted John.

'I'm very comfortable, thank you,' said John.

'Of course you've been through all this before,' said his visitor.

John just started to recognise him, from the press conference he'd given on that afternoon outside the hotel.

'Not at Lewes.'

'They'll probably move you to Wandsworth or Brixton – you're too big a fish for this small pond. They're making me a cup of tea - do you want one?'

His visitor went over to the door, gestured through the glass, and came back to the table. 'Somerfield – *News of the World*,' he announced, sticking out a hand.

'Oh yes, you wrote to me,' said John.

'I think we could have a mutual interest in your case. Who've you got fixed up as a brief to defend you?'

'I told the court I'd get something arranged by next week. They offered me legal aid.'

There was a knock on the door with the tea. Somerfield brought it back and placed it in front of John. 'Legal aid's fine but you don't know quite who you're going to get. Why not leave it to us, all expenses paid: solicitors, barristers, psychos, someone to clean your shoes in the morning, the lot.'

'What's in it for you, then?'

'Your life story, Mr Haigh. Start to finish. Anything special about your childhood and upbringing, your victims and why you bumped them off. I understand you're a man of faith so you could tell us a bit about your religious views. That sort of thing. We'll run it in a few episodes after the trial is over. If the worst happens, it'll start after you're sentenced – if you go to Broadmoor, it'll start then.'

'How I became a vampire, perhaps, according to the *Daily Mirror*?'

'Are you doing anything about them? After all, this could seriously affect your case. You need to get an injunction out against them, contempt of court I'd say. The sooner we sort this out with your legal team the better.'

John took a sip of his tea and accepted a cigarette. 'I do have religious beliefs, as a matter of fact. My parents were strict Plymouth Brethren and we didn't have newspapers or the wireless or frivolities like that. Then I was a choirboy at Wakefield Cathedral, which was High Church, crucifixes, the full works. I don't know why they let me go there. I wonder if they really knew where I was going those Sunday mornings.'

'How have they taken all this?'

'Badly, especially my mother. But I think they see it all like Wakefield Cathedral, on the other side of the fence, part of my corruption by the world outside. Well, that's as may be, but what I believe is that it's all pre-ordained, it's God's will and if I was marked as a killer from the start there was little I could do about it. I can face death if I have to.'

'Even if you have caused death?'

'Remember Christ lived off the people. He didn't have to work, they were glad to give. As a chosen one I have chosen to live off the people, whether it's hire purchase for cars, shares they didn't need anyway or their houses and everything else they own.'

'But you never gave them the choice, Mr Haigh. That's the difference.'

'I don't think you understand. Had they known what was to happen, they would have given gladly. These people were my friends, in the cases of Mac and Archie Henderson, my intimate friends. They loved me and I loved them.'

Somerfield, for the first time that afternoon, looked uncomfortable. 'What are you saying, Mr Haigh? We run a respectable newspaper at *News of the World*.'

'You're also man of the world, Mr Somerfield. But you can have your story.'

'I don't want an editor getting funny about it because he thinks you're queer, that's all. Quickest way to lose readers, I'm afraid.'

John laughed. 'There's someone else. There's a girl called Barbara. I'd like to pass on to her anything you pay me.'

'So you have a girlfriend.'

'But I want to make it clear I respected her too much to take it beyond a platonic relationship. She's only young, half my age, but she'll be able to go into a new life.'

'Blimey, I didn't think there were people like you left,' said Somerfield.

John got back to business. 'What about the attorney general for my defence, would he be too much? I do have a doctor in mind, a psychiatrist from Harley Street.'

'Oh yes, who's that?'

'A name like Yellowknees.'

'Yellowlees. Yes, I've seen him in action. He knows his stuff.'

'Let's hope he can swing it. I'm more use to you in Broadmoor than, er, the alternative.'

'That's right, but just in case get all the writing done by the trial, if you would. There is one thing, I hear you've said there were three more victims.'

'Oh, yes. Don't take too much notice of them. I told them six when I came in here. No one will be able to prove it one way or the other.'

'They also found a body near the Lagonda when it went over the cliff at Beachy Head.'

'That's right. Now let's be clear about that. The Lagonda was mine and I got the insurance on that. But the body was nothing to do with me – that was just coincidence. If that had been me, it would probably be in my interest to own up to it now.'

Somerfield was now making a few notes in a flip-over notebook. His initial hardboiled impression of an American private investigator was softening in the presence of so many bodies and written-off cars. 'Will you be seeing your parents at all?' he asked.

'No, they're rather elderly for all this. It would finish Mum off. She wouldn't want to see her son the sinner. Do you know when I was a boy Dad used to explain a blue scar on his forehead as there because he was a sinner. When I asked him why Mum hadn't got a mark, he said it was because she was an angel.'

'Did he say what sins had brought that on?'

'In the end I found out he'd had an accident at the colliery where he worked and that left him with a scar. But for years I thought every time I did something naughty the mark would appear. Of course when I found out it didn't then that was full steam ahead with whatever I wanted to do. See, there's nothing there.'

John leant forward to show an unblemished and carefully combed forehead that had been thoroughly tested over the last five years.

'I could see your parents, if you like. Say I've seen you and that sort of thing.'

John wrote out the address in Outwood, Leeds, for him on his notepad. 'Thanks, that would be nice. I don't want them plastered over the newspaper, if you don't mind, but they would appreciate seeing you. They haven't been down to London so you'd have to go up there. Assuming they see you, of course. I'll write to them and tell them to expect you.'

Somerfield started to get to his feet. 'Well, if there's nothing else, I'd better be going. We'll meet again.'

'There is one other thing you can do for me,' John added.

'Of course,' said Somerfield, ready to give his client anything after granting him and his newspaper one of the major scoops ever in crime reporting.

'Give me a lift down to the station,' John giggled. 'They've impounded my car at Chelsea Police Station.'

The last thing John did that day was to sit down and write to Barbara. The sight of her on the previous day, convulsed on the opposite side of the glass in the visitors' room, had penetrated even to him.

Using Mrs Durand-Deacon's pen, which he'd kept after disposing of her, he wrote:

Lewes Prison

4.3.49

Barbara Darling,

   Many thanks for coming to see me yesterday. It grieves me that it was such a shocking ordeal for you. I suppose no one knows better than you how difficult it is to upset my calm; but I can assure you that irrespective of my superficial appearance I was very badly shaken. I have never in my life seen a face so utterly convulsed in sheer agony of sorrow. And what could I do about it with a large sheet of glass between us. Darling if only I could have met you normally I would have left no doubt in your mind as to whether the last 5 years have meant anything to me or not. Surely you must know that I have loved you intensely during that time.

How foolish of you to ask why I hadn't murdered you. Of course I had millions of opportunities, I know that. But the idea never even crossed my mind. I wouldn't have hurt a hair on your head.

The other business is something entirely separate and different. There was no affection involved there. I know the papers talked of 6 widows but they haven't got the whole story yet. There were men as well as women but how many I don't know, probably a dozen or more, and it was not their money but their blood that I wanted. You were very perceptive yesterday. You did really sum up the position rightly. These two things had to go together.

It was so kind of you to ask if you should write to my mother. Yes I think you should. I'd like you to and the greater kindness would be to explain what you told me yesterday. Not that you thought it was her fault but about the people about whom I used to laugh. She's taken that better than anything else.

Darling I can't go on discussing these two alien things side by side. I have loved you – and still do and it has been beautiful. I don't ask the converse, I know that you have loved me as with an intensity which was beyond all doubt.

When this episode is over you must forget me and start your life again.

I grieve that I cannot continue it without you. Bless you for coming and for all you have ever done for me and meant to me.

My eternal gratitude to Jimmy for looking after you at this time.

And now my undying love as always since I have known you.

John.

20

Up to the time of his meeting with Somerfield, John Haigh had regarded the *Daily Mirror*'s reporting of the case as rather a joke, something that might in fact considerably help persuade a jury that he was insane and needed to be sent to Broadmoor for treatment – with a good chance of being released sooner or later. This was what he'd had in mind when he put the question to Inspector Webb as he was about to make his confession in Chelsea Police Station.

On 3 March 1949, the day before the Somerfield meeting at the prison, the *Daily Mirror* ran the front-page headline 'Vampire Horror in Notting Hill', with an account of the mysterious disappearance of Dr and Mrs Henderson and Mr and Mrs McSwan and their son. 'The Yard believes that the vampire maniac wiped out five people – two well-to-do London families – and then dismembered and destroyed their bodies.' On the same page was a photograph of John leaving Horsham Magistrates' Court and photographs of Dr and Mrs Henderson, who were described as 'victims of the vampire'.

The next day accounts of the vampire killer continued with the headline 'Vampire – A Man Held' and 'Vampire Confesses', along with a description of John and how he'd killed five people and was now awaiting trial for other offences. If that wasn't enough, the article went on to describe him disposing of the bodies by 'acid cremation'.

All this followed a warning the previous day by a worried Scotland Yard:

A report has been published today that New Scotland Yard is investigating a case in which a vampire murderer drinks his victims' blood. The only statement on this matter which has been made to the police under caution is in a case which is now *sub judice.* That statement may be offered in evidence, and any stories that refer to that statement or its contents may be held to prejudice the trial of the accused. Publication of any such statement or references to it would be most improper, and would doubtless become a matter for consideration of the Court before whom the accused appears.

True to their word, the *News of the World* had gone ahead and appointed a legal team to represent their new client. The solicitor chosen was a local man, Mr Ireland Eager, senior partner in a Horsham firm and, while an experienced solicitor in mainly non-contentious areas such as conveyancing and probate, he was less experienced in criminal cases. He was now landed with one of the most notorious serial murder cases of the century, with implications of insanity pleas, similar fact evidence, boxes full of statements and exhibits, and a legal argument as to whether the case should be tried at the Old Bailey or the home court at Lewes. On top of all this was now the tricky question of whether to start proceedings against a national newspaper for contempt of court or whether that should be left to the Director of Public Prosecutions. In the long run, would it be better just to ignore the *Daily Mirror* and other newspapers, which would inevitably follow the story with similar headlines, in case more publicity was stirred up for the client, whose notoriety probably already prevented him having a fair trial anyway?

In short, this was a case most country solicitors would run from and with good reason, especially since the contempt application with supporting affidavits and exhibits had to be filed and served at breakneck speed. These would be heard by the Lord Chief Justice of England and the High Court judge who was eventually to try the case.

In the event it was decided that the application for contempt should go ahead, and Sir Walter Monckton KC was briefed to lead the application. Monckton had already achieved fame as Edward VIII's legal advisor during the abdication crisis in 1936 and conducted negotiations with the then prime minister, Stanley Baldwin. He became solicitor general in 1945 in Churchill's caretaker government.

Mr Silvester Bolam, editor of the *Daily Mirror*, was brought before the court on 21 March 1949 and counsel for Bolam said he was there to admit a great error and to tender Bolam's most humble apologies to the court. In mitigation, Bolam said at the time he thought it was no contempt of court provided no charge had been made against anyone in connection with the missing persons and provided no one was alleged to be responsible for their disappearance. The court was also reminded of the way in which a modern newspaper is produced and how errors of judgement can occur. An unimpressed Lord Goddard, as Lord Chief Justice, replied it was not an error of judgement but a question of policy, and that what had been written were the most horrifying things one could possibly read.

The directors of the company that owned the *Daily Mirror* were brought before the court. Bolam, as editor, was sent to Brixton prison for three months, the company was fined the unprecedented amount of £10,000 and costs and the directors were warned that if for the purpose of increasing the circulation of their newspaper they again published such matter, they might find the arm of the court long enough to reach them and deal with them individually.

In his judgement Lord Goddard said:

Anybody who has had the misfortune, as this Court has had, to read these articles must be left wondering how it would be possible for that man to obtain a fair trial after that which has been published in this paper. Not only does it describe him as a vampire and proceed to give reasons why they call him a vampire, but, in addition to saying that he has been charged with the particular murder with which he has been charged, these articles go on to say, not merely that he is charged with other murders, but that he had committed other murders and to give the names of persons who they said he has murdered and a photograph of a person whom he is said to have murdered, and to describe the way she was murdered.

In the long history of this class of case there has, in the opinion of this Court, never been a case approaching the gravity as this or one of such a scandalous and wicked character. It is of the utmost importance that the Court should vindicate the common principles of justice and in the public interest see that condign punishment is meted out to persons guilty of such conduct.

John Haigh had already been transferred to Brixton prison to be remanded awaiting his trial for two weeks when Silvester Bolam arrived to take up his place in the same prison.

21

John's transfer to Brixton had been ordered by the Horsham magistrates on 11 March at one of their remand hearings because the hospital wing of Lewes prison, which primarily housed young offenders, was considered unsuitable for a prisoner likely to be on remand for several weeks. His legal team had no objection and nor did John, and it would make visits for London-based counsel and doctors more convenient, but less so for Barbara and John's solicitor, Mr Eager.

What John found on the remand wing at Brixton were special conditions for those on capital charges similar to an old-fashioned public school, with beds set out dormitory-style in a room the size of a hospital ward, and a table in the middle at which prisoners sat for meals or to read or write, or perhaps take recreation in the form of board games or cards. For John there was a sociability about the place, as there was in the Onslow Court Hotel: there were fellow residents to chat to during meals or afterwards, if he wasn't searching through law books out of the prison library or writing his life story for the *News of the World* on sheets of foolscap paper. He was even allowed to bring in his hairdresser, George Burge, who'd cut his hair for the last three years at the Grosvenor Hotel, Victoria.

This was also the opportunity for observation by a medical team as to a prisoner's mental state and reports were prepared for the court. Such medical reports could play a vital role in deciding whether a prisoner might be sent to Broadmoor Hospital – or the Broadmoor Institution as it was still known – and would, at the very least, help visiting psychiatrists called to give expert evidence in preparing their own reports for defence teams and the court.

From the start it was obvious that John was going to be found guilty of the murder of Olive Durand-Deacon: he'd confessed to it and given a graphic description of how he killed her and disposed of the body. Furthermore, everything he'd said tallied with the police investigation, indeed had been helpful to the investigation in putting together the pieces of the jigsaw as to what happened from the moment Mrs Durand-Deacon left the hotel until she was 'converted' a few days later into a sludge and deposited in the yard at Leopold Road.

What wasn't proving easy for the defence team was finding a doctor who thought John was mad, or at least sufficiently mad to be considered as suffering from a 'disease of the mind' under the M'Naghten Rules. These rules set out the requirements for the defence of insanity that would help him escape the rope. Each doctor would carefully read the police statements and the reports put together by the prison medical team, interview John himself and then write his own report. And every time a report dropped on to the desk of Mr Eager, John's solicitor, he came to the conclusion that while there were undoubtedly mental issues, they did not amount to insanity or a 'disease of the mind' needed under the M'Naghten Rules.

Doctors Desmond Curran and J.R. Rees both examined John in the last week of March and first week of April on behalf of the defence and both came to the conclusion that he was sane and fit to stand trial. They also discussed the case with Dr Matheson, who thought no further opinion was needed at that stage from an expert on the question of John's sanity.

In writing to Mr Eager on 13 April and enclosing further notes for Curran and Rees, John managed to find a cause of his own. He asked his solicitor to send a telegram on his behalf to a Mrs Duffey, who apparently had been under a sentence of death in Strangeways prison, Manchester, saying: 'Heartfelt joy at news of the reprieve. Fervently hope King grants pardon. You have suffered anguish enough.'

John then added in the letter:

I think we should not forget other people's sorrow amidst our own troubles and I do think this poor girl has suffered terribly. She should never have had to go through this ordeal. It was so patent what should happen from the beginning. Truly as Dickens said the law is an ass.

Doctors giving expert evidence in court are notorious for not being able to agree on the medical evidence, but in this case there was unanimity among the psychiatrists that John George Haigh was sane and putting on an act of drinking his victims' blood and having colourful dreams about trees dripping with blood in order to get to Broadmoor, a situation hardly helped by Haigh himself when he'd asked Inspector Webb what his chances were of getting out of Broadmoor.

Dr Matheson, meanwhile, as head of the prison team of psychiatrists, had been able to watch John on a daily basis and speak to Barbara Stephens. He wrote up his report on 26 April 1949 when he found that John's mother had been a great student of dreams and had brought books into the house, books that John was allowed to read, on how dreams foretold the future. John told him that he'd been mischievous at school and had no real friends there, although he was not unpopular just as he was not popular.

As to sex, at 20 John had been introduced to it by a friend and for six years lived a loose and free life, but then the opposite sex became 'repugnant to him' sexually after 1940.

John told him he liked keeping his hands clean and wore gloves, even in summer. He said he never had any real affection for his victims.

His IQ was average to superior, and he'd got a great thrill out of the publicity to do with the case.

Dr Matheson was not satisfied John had drunk blood; anyway, John was not up on the pathology of bleeding, which in Dr Matheson's view would last up to one hour when the jugular vein is cut. John had also given different accounts on how long the bleeding took. Dr Matheson considered John did not have the dream about cruciforms and blood, and showed a desire to make the whole story dramatic.

A Rorschach Assessment, a psychological test in which the subject's reactions to inkblots are recorded and analysed –in John's case, they were sent to the Maudsley Hospital in London for analysis – was also carried out in Brixton at this time. The assessment found that the subject had above average intelligence but, resisting a drab and ordinary existence, lived in a world of fantasy and had lost touch with the common aspects and problems of life. Maudsley, not knowing his identity, found an amazing lack of emotional feeling in the subject, who seemed to view human beings as fantastic and ridiculous. The language of the subject was 'sanguinary', with images of slaughter and blood suggesting murder preoccupations contemplated or murder actually committed.

After two unhelpful reports from specialist consultants, and no fewer than four prison doctors coming to the same conclusion, the defence team changed tactics. They briefed a certain Dr Henry Yellowlees, who'd worked at St Thomas's Hospital in London as a psychiatrist and lecturer for many years, saying two of his colleagues had found the patient to be sane and they would now like his views, in effect throwing down the gauntlet to disagree with their conclusion.

What wasn't on the defence's side was time; after all the comings and goings of the first two doctors, each of whom had to read all the material, see John in Brixton a few times and liaise all the while with the prison doctors, Dr Yellowlees was left with a little over two weeks to go through the same process, although nearly four months had now passed from John's arrest.

The pressure of time had already made Sir David Maxwell Fyfe, now appointed as leading counsel for the defence, to make an application to the court to postpone the trial, with one rather unexpected result. While Haigh had not got the attorney general, Sir Hartley Shawcross – leading for the prosecution – on his side, Maxwell Fyfe was a former attorney general with a distinguished record as a prosecutor under Hartley Shawcross at the Nuremburg Trials during the Second World War.

The application came up on 27 April in front of Mr Justice Travers Humphreys, who was already familiar with the case after sitting on the bench at the contempt hearing against the *Daily Mirror*. Humphreys, coming up to his eighty-second birthday and a judge for over twenty years, was impressed neither by the application to delay the trial nor the idea that the Old Bailey was the right choice of venue to hold the trial. Without mincing his words, he said that this case was nothing to do with the Old Bailey as it was about a murder in Sussex and should be tried in Sussex and that the Old Bailey had become 'a dumping ground' for criminal trials from all over the country. In sending the case down to the next Lewes Assizes, it was already known that Mr Justice Humphreys would be presiding there and so John Haigh would be tried by him, adding another notorious name to the trials over which he had presided or taken part as a barrister, to include those of Oscar Wilde, Dr Crippen, Roger Casement and George 'Brides in the Bath' Smith.

In transferring the case to Lewes, the judge was in effect allowing a postponement of the trial as the next assizes in Lewes were two months away, giving the doctors time to sort themselves out, John time reflect on how he was to play the trial and his lawyers a chance to take a deep breath.

The time for quiet reflection for John ended two days later when there was a scream from the bed next to him in the middle of the night.

22

Things had almost settled into a routine on the remand wing at Brixton when Martin threw his first fit. There were letters for John to write to his parents, Barbara and one or two friends; there was even a reply to be made to an enquiry from a member of the public asking if he might 'borrow' John's Alvis while he was inside as John would have no use for it at the moment and it had always been his ambition to have a car like that. John, in his usual way, said he would be delighted if he could get the permission of the police but thought this unlikely as the car was still in mothballs at Chelsea Police Station. In a way it was one good turn deserving another as John had originally bought the car on HP but then 'sold' it several times when he was short of money, before renting it back to himself so he could carry on using it. He'd lost track of who the present owner was, so whoever was writing to him might as well have it anyway.

John had already got to know Martin over the first few days he was transferred to Brixton. In fact it was hard not to get to know Martin, whether you wanted to or not, as he was in the habit of ranging around the room asking if he might have a cigarette, telling you his life story and how, as a mixed-race kid, he'd been adopted by a clergyman and his wife to come and live with their four children in a large rectory in the depths of the Kent countryside. He'd left school early and been classified as unfit to serve in the army for the war, or for anything else much. His career in crime had even failed, and then he'd killed a friend in a fight over a bottle of beer.

Martin wanted to know about Barbara as John sat at the long table in the centre of the room, writing his daily letter to her.

'Is she lovely?' he asked.

Mrs Olive Durand-Deacon, John Haigh's sixth victim. (Dunboyne, Lord (ed.), *The Trial of John George Haigh*)

The Onslow Court Hotel, Kensington, home to John Haigh and his victim Mrs Durand-Deacon. (Somerfield, S., *Haigh*)

Mrs Robbie, manageress of the Onslow Court Hotel, Mrs Kirkwood, her head cashier, and Mrs Constance Lane, friend of Mrs Durand-Deacon, arrive to give evidence in court. (Somerfield, S., *Haigh*)

Haigh's workshop in Leopold Road, Crawley. (Dunboyne, Lord (ed.) *The Trial of John George Haigh*)

Haigh's order for a carboy of sulphuric acid to 'convert' Mrs Durand-Deacon. (Dunboyne, Lord (ed.), *The Trial of John George Haigh*)

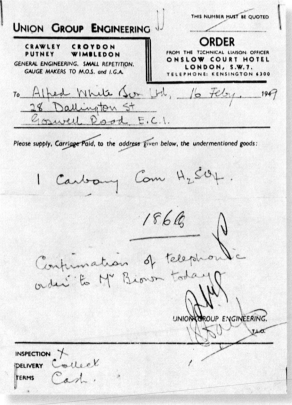

Haigh's protective outfit when handling acid to dispose of bodies, as modelled by a police officer. (*Murder in Mind* magazine)

John Haigh at the wheel of his beloved Alvis.
(La Bern, A., *Haigh – The Mind of a Murderer*)

Barbara Stephens, John Haigh's faithful companion
for five years. (National Archives)

The inside of the workroom at Leopold Road, Crawley. (Dunboyne, Lord (ed.),
The Trial of John George Haigh)

The dining room in the Onslow Court Hotel as it is today. (Author's collection)

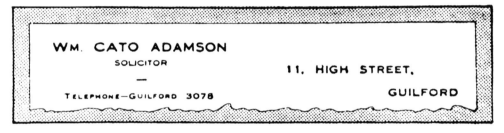

WM. CATO ADAMSON
SOLICITOR
—
TELEPHONE—GUILFORD 3078

11, HIGH STREET,
GUILFORD

Letter heading used by Haigh posing as a solicitor but misspelling Guildford. (National Archives)

Haigh's desk at the Crawley factory, as he left it. (National Archives)

The Enfield revolver used by Haigh to shoot Mrs Durand-Deacon, Dr and Mrs Henderson. The revolver belonged to Dr Henderson. (*Murder in Mind* magazine)

Receipt from Cottage Cleaners of Reigate for Mrs Durand-Deacon's Persian lamb coat. The assistant didn't think Haigh the type whose wife would be able to afford such a coat. (Dunboyne, Lord (ed.), *The Trial of John George Haigh*)

Donald McSwan, Haigh's first London employer and first victim. (Dunboyne, Lord (ed.), *The Trial of John George Haigh*)

Above left: The entrance to the basement at No. 79 Gloucester Road. (Somerfield, S., *Haigh*)

Above right: The drain in the basement of No. 79 Gloucester Road, down which Haigh disposed of the remains of Donald McSwan and his parents. (Somerfield, S., *Haigh*)

Dr and Mrs Henderson, successful doctor and socialite, who both fell prey to Haigh. (National Archives)

Sgt Maude Lambourne. (With kind permission of Heather Johnston and Erica Hare)

Police with boxes of soil at the storeroom yard at Leopold Road, Crawley, for sifting by Dr Simpson, the pathologist. Chief Inspector Mahon is third from left and Inspector Symes fourth from left. (*Murder in Mind* magazine)

John Haigh's room, in what was then the Onslow Court Hotel, as it is today. (Author's collection)

Haigh's famous 'shopping list' of items to dispose of Mrs Durand-Deacon. (Dunboyne, Lord (ed.), *The Trial of John George Haigh*)

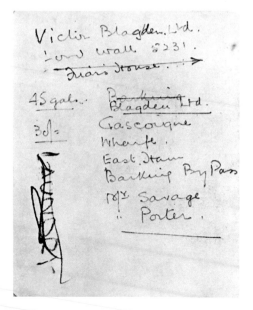

Haigh as a boy. (Dunboyne, Lord (ed.), *The Trial of John George Haigh*)

Haigh arrives at court in Horsham, watched by a good turnout of locals. (Somerfield, S., *Haigh*)

The Alvis. (*Murder in Mind* magazine)

The front page of the *Daily Mirror* on 3 March 1949. (The British Library)

Barbara Stephens watches Haigh driven away from court by the police. (*Daily Express*, 19 July 1949)

Daily Mirror

FRI MAR. 4 1949

ONE PENNY

No. 14,095

Registered at G.P.O. as a Newspaper.

FORWARD WITH THE PEOPLE

THE VAMPIRE CONFESSES

THE Vampire Killer will never strike again. He is safely behind bars, powerless ever again to lure his victims to a hideous death.

This is the assurance which the *Daily Mirror* can give today. It is the considered conclusion of the finest detective brains in the country.

IT WAS A WOMAN'S HUNCH THAT TRAPPED HIM

A WOMAN'S intuition first put the police on the trail of the Vampire.

It was that intuition that made Woman Police-Sergeant Maud Lambourne study the "missing persons" file at her police station recently.

And the same sixth sense made her decide to investigate a report personally, although there seemed nothing unusual. Similar reports are filed three times a week at her station.

She put routine questions. She put them to a man. Her intuition told her she was no longer investigating a disappearance. It was murder.

Maud Lambourne went back to her station, where the C.I.D. had come to respect her intuition.

They knew already held four commendations from the Chief Commissioner of Scotland Yard for her detective work.

They listened—and took over the investigation.

From that moment the story of the greatest series of murders since Palmer the Poisoner, nearly a hundred years ago, began to crystallise in the test tubes of the Scotland Yard scientists.

Police-Sergeant Lambourne, eight years in the Force, has played her part.

DEFENCE: PREMIER TO SEE CHURCHILL

MR. ATTLEE revealed last night that he is ready to give Mr. Churchill details of our defences— but Mr. Churchill has not so far informed me of the time when he would see me."

The Government, he added, are advised that in present conditions a great deal of information should not be released.

War of science will not find us unready—Page 7.

The full tally of the Vampire's crimes is still not known.

It will take squads of police many weeks to test the ghastly tale which has come tumbling from his own lips as he sat, wild-eyed and drawn, under a powerful guard.

But as the police have listened appalled, to his sadistic story of mass murder, mutilation and the drinking of his victims' blood, confirmation has been flashed back of his earlier boasts.

During the interrogation the monster explained that he was not happy about the first murders.

"It was a messy business," he said. "I found that my technique improved later."

It was as if a great artist were looking back on his handiwork.

He told his questioners that he cut the throats of the people he had killed, and sucked their blood through a lemonade straw.

And so far he has named on his catalogue of murder five people only. They are:—

Dr. Archibald Henderson;

Mrs. Rosalie Mercy Henderson, his wife;

Mr. Donald McSwan;

Mrs. Amy McSwan, his wife; and

Mr. Donald John McSwan, their son.

Dr. and Mrs. Henderson disappeared in February of last year.

Mr. Donald McSwan, property owner, and his family, of Kenilworth-avenue, Wimbledon, S.W., vanished three years or more ago.

Genteel

Hour after hour, to relays of detectives and shorthand writers crowded into the buff-painted interrogation room of a London police station, the Vampire has recalled his orgies.

Drinking mug after mug of strong police tea—but never forgetting to crook his little finger genteelly away from the coarse china—the maniac has shown himself a man of easy manners.

He wears a quiet suit, of immaculate cut, with a discreet tie. His hair is sleekly brushed, his nails well-kept.

From the interrogation room he has now gone back to his cell. Here he is already awaiting trial for other offences.

The Director of Public Prosecutions now awaits police and medical reports before deciding on what action the Crown shall take.

Scotland Yard men working on the dossier of the McSwan family had by last night put together the final pieces of a strange jigsaw.

Mr. and Mrs. Donald Mc-

Continued on Back Page

Kept alive a month to sign killer's notes?

Mrs. Rosalie Henderson, 41, victim of the Vampire murderer. Last night her brother said: "I am convinced she was kept under duress and forced to sign letters for a month before she was shot." Story on Back Page.

Advertiser's Announcement

Reduced Prices of FRY'S Chocolates

As from February 27th all Fry's chocolates are reduced in price or increased in weight. Better value. Quality unchanged.

FRY'S NEW PRICES

Sandwich Assortment	1/- ¼lb. ctn.
Silver Lining Assortment	1/2 ¼lb. ctn.
Crunchie	4d. each
Chocolate Cream	2d. & 3½d. each
Sandwich Block	5d. each
Quality ½lb. Block	11d. each

FRY'S MAKERS OF GOOD CHOCOLATE

No. 79—room of horror

In tins, bags and little parcels, detectives bring specimens from the back-basement of 79, Gloucester-road, London, S.W., in which the McSwans are believed to have been slain, Police digging, found false teeth in the floor.

3 thirsty Russians rush the barricade

THREE of the eight Russian officials besieged in a Frankfurt building by American troops broke from the building last night.

Ignoring calls to halt and the glare of searchlights, they dashed to a garage behind the building and tried to start up a car. American military police sent them back into the building.

The officials have been ordered by the Russian authorities to return to the Soviet Zone, Berlin radio said last night.

Gas, light and water services to the building have been cut off. The phones have been disconnected, and no food is being allowed in.

His booby trap tripped the wrong man

SAT ON HIM

Evans, of Bryn Hirgoed, Glam. was described by the judge as being "quite capable of looking after herself" in a physical contest with her husband, a small man.

She wept when her husband, Ernest Rees Evans, a chemist, was awarded a decree on the ground of cruelty.

The front page of the *Daily Mirror* on 4 March 1949. (Dunboyne, Lord (ed.), *The Trial of John George Haigh*)

Mr Justice Humphreys, whose summing-up to the jury Haigh described as 'masterly'. (Dunboyne, Lord (ed.), *The Trial of John George Haigh*)

Far left: Sir Hartley Shawcross KC, MP, leading counsel for the prosecution. (Dunboyne, Lord (ed.), *The Trial of John George Haigh*)

Left: Dr Henry Yellowlees, the only witness for the defence. (Somerfield, S., *Haigh*)

VISITING ORDER WANDSWORTH.
H. M. Prison,
4 . 8 . 49 . 19
Reg. No. 7663 Name Haigh JG.
has permission to be visited by Mr Sommerfield
℅ News of the World 30 Bouverie St Fleet St
EC4.

1. The visit to last only 30 minutes.
2. Visitors admitted only between the hours of 1.30 p.m. and 3.30 p.m.
3. No Visit allowed on Sundays, Christmas Day, or Good Friday.
4. Such of the above-named friends who wish to visit, must all attend at the same time, and produce this order.

Governor

Above: Stafford Somerfield's visiting order to see John Haigh in his last days at Wandsworth Prison. (Somerfield, S., *Haigh*)

Above: Sir David Maxwell Fyfe KC, MP, leading counsel for the defence, with junior counsel Mr G.R.F. Morris. (Dunboyne, Lord (ed.), *The Trial of John George Haigh*)

Right: Haigh's last note to Stafford Somerfield, written on the night before his execution. (The British Library)

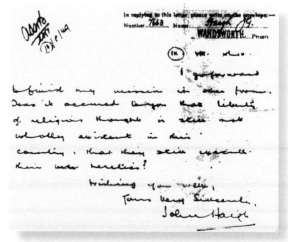

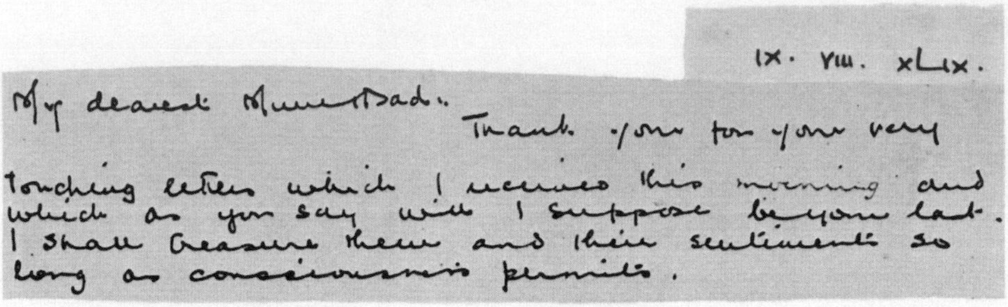

IX. VIII. XLIX.

My dearest Mum & Dad..

Thank you for your very touching letter which I received this morning and which as you say will I suppose be your last. I shall treasure them and their sentiments so long as consciousness permits.

The handwriting perhaps betrays a sense of urgency, but the words are still confident and affectionate . . .

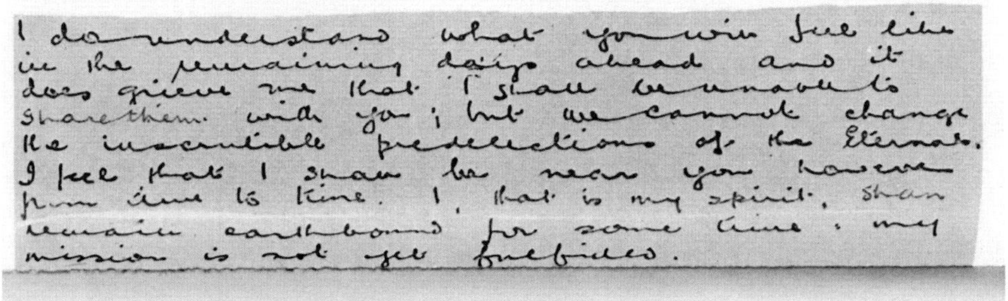

I do understand what you will feel like in the remaining days ahead and it does grieve me that I shall be unable to share them with you; but we cannot change the inscrutible predelictions of the Eternal. I feel that I shall be near you however from time to time. I, that is my spirit, shall remain earthbound for some time: my mission is not yet fulfilled.

He closed: 'Please give my love to everybody and thank them on my behalf for their kindly solicitations . . .

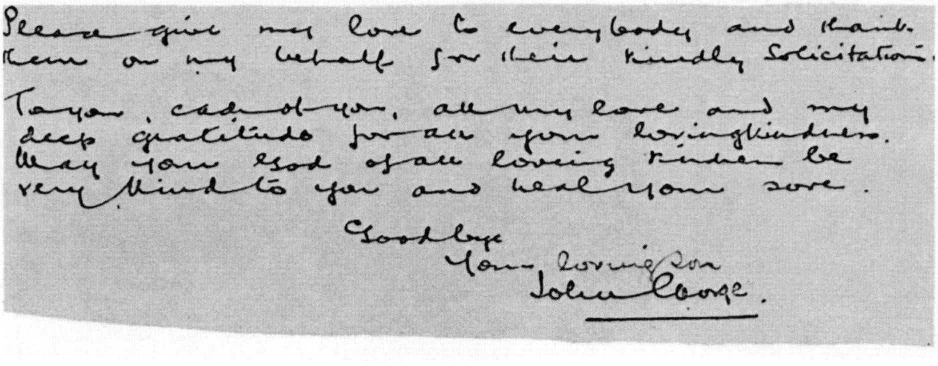

Please give my love to everybody and thank them on my behalf for their kindly solicitation.

To you, each of you, all my love and my deep gratitude for all your lovingkindness. May your God of all loving kindness be very kind to you and heal your sore.

Goodbye

Your loving son

John George.

John Haigh's last letter to his parents on the eve of his execution. (La Bern, A., *Haigh – The Mind of a Murderer*)

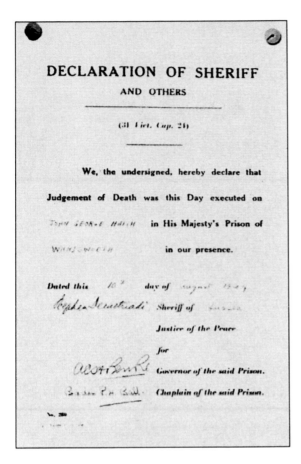

DECLARATION OF SHERIFF
AND OTHERS

(31 Vict. Cap. 21)

We, the undersigned, hereby declare that

Judgement of Death was this Day executed on

John George Haigh in His Majesty's Prison of

Wandsworth in our presence.

Dated this *10* day of *August 1949*

[signature] Sheriff of *Sussex*

Justice of the Peace

for

[signature] Governor of the said Prison.

[signature] Chaplain of the said Prison.

No. 280

Left: Declaration of Death signed by the sheriff, the prison governor and the chaplain, posted on the prison doors after John Haigh's execution. (*Murder in Mind* magazine)

Below left: A large crowd of 500 people, including a group of schoolgirls and a man in a wheelchair, awaits outside Wandsworth prison for news of the execution in a holiday atmosphere. (Somerfield, S., *Haigh*)

Below: John Haigh lives on in the Chamber of Horrors at Madame Tussauds. A life mask was made in the death cell on the day before his execution and the waxwork then dressed in his own clothes. (Dunboyne, Lord (ed.), *The Trial of John George Haigh*)

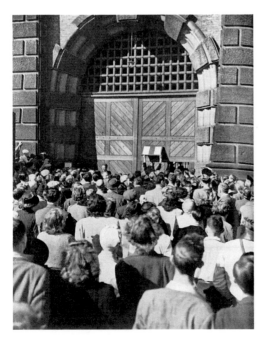

John Haigh's longhand list of his 'nine victims' for his *News of the World* story, complete with methods of disposal. (The British Library)

Part of John Haigh's draft for the *News of the World* story denying that his motive was financial gain. (The British Library)

Tel No.: WHItehall 8100

Ext...............

Any communication on the subject of this letter should be addressed to:—

THE UNDER SECRETARY OF STATE, HOME OFFICE, LONDON, S.W.1

and the following number quoted—

815319/19

Your Ref...................

P24154/18

PRISON COMMISSION

8 - AUG 1949

HOME OFFICE,

WHITEHALL.

6th August, 1949.

Sir,

I am directed to inform you that, having carefully considered all the circumstances of the case of John George Haigh, now lying under sentence of death in Wandsworth Prison, and having caused a special Medical Inquiry to be made as to the prisoner's mental condition by Sir Norwood East, Dr. J. S. Hopwood and Dr. H. T. P. Young, under Section 2(4) of the Criminal Lunatics Act, 1884, the Secretary of State has been unable to find any sufficient ground to justify him in advising His Majesty to interfere with the due course of law.

I am, Sir,

Your obedient Servant,

J. aNewsam

The Secretary,
    Prison Commission,
        Horseferry House,
            Dean Ryle Street,
                S.W.1.

Letter from the Home Office on 6 August 1949 refusing John Haigh a reprieve. (National Archives)

John Haigh leaves court with his police escort. (National Archives)

Studio portrait of John Haigh posing as a socialite. (National Archives)

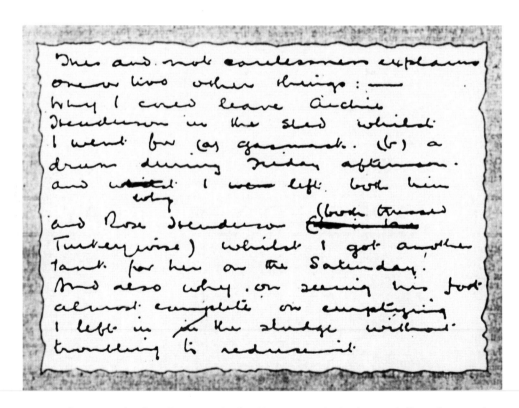

A page from Haigh's handwritten draft of his story which shows chilling disregard for his victims. (National Archives)

'She is, but then she's half my age,' said John.

'Does what she's told, then?'

'Most of the time, but she has a mind of her own.'

Martin lowered his voice. 'My wife had a mind of her own. We had a child. She had the boy adopted and went to Australia. What do you think of that? If I get through this I'm going to have the boy live with me and give him a life. Least I can do, I reckon.' He accepted a cigarette. 'What about you?'

'We'd only been married about four months, when she upped and left. I was twenty-five and it was the only way I was going to get out of home. Betty had the child adopted as well. Mind you, it didn't help me going into prison, I can't blame her. I'm not even sure the child was mine – according to my calculations it would have been conceived after I went into prison. It was a little girl, Pauline. I never saw either of them again. It put me off women.'

'What about Barbara?' asked Martin.

'We had tea together, went to shows and listened to music. That was it, nothing more. May be just as well, she can start a new life now, whatever happens to me.'

'What do think will happen to you?'

John put down his, or rather Mrs Durand-Deacon's, pen and thought about this. 'I reckon Broadmoor. I've told them about the dreams I get and drinking blood, that sort of thing. Should be enough, although it hasn't worked so far. They've looked at me and say I'm okay. What about you?'

'Well, I've a bit of a history. Been in and out of a few hospitals, including the medical wing in this place. You've got to be careful, though. Just because you kill someone doesn't mean you're mad.'

'I've killed six; well, nine according to what I've said, but it's six, between you and me.'

'So you are the vampire, then. We weren't quite sure. You look a bit too respectable to have got up to all that.'

Martin stood, solemnly shook him by the hand and then sat down again. 'I don't know if I should have a bed next to you, though. I mean, what happens if you got thirsty in the night?'

'I am respectable,' John laughed. 'Most of the time.'

'Has it made you rich, that's the thing?'

'Most of the time,' repeated John.

They tried playing a game of draughts but Martin couldn't concentrate for more than a couple of moves and had to carry on walking around the room.

He would stop at another prisoner and talk to him about Wandsworth or the West Country, where it was easier and where he'd take his young son when he got out and give him the sort of life he deserved after his mother deserted him for Australia and how glad he was she didn't take him there because the place was full of criminals.

But at about two in the morning John, always a good sleeper, was aroused from his slumbers by a penetrating and high-pitched scream from the bed next to him. John could just make out Martin writhing around in his bed, tearing at his sheets and pummelling his pillow as if it was a live thing. The scream didn't sound like Martin, who now wasn't helped by a mouth full of sheet that he chewed and bit as if his life depended on it.

For a moment or two nothing much happened, except for some cursing from other beds and threats to come over and shut him up for good. The duty screw, sitting at the table where he and his colleagues kept an all-night vigil, writing reports or reading newspapers under a dim table light with a green shade, looked up but took no further action. When it was obvious the noise was not going to stop, he stood up and called through the door for help. Eventually the main lights came on, with more cursing and swearing from the prisoners, while two white-coated orderlies breezed in and took up positions either side of Martin's bed. One of the orderlies took the sheet out of his mouth and gave him a slap across the face. This subdued the patient long enough for the other orderly to stick a syringe into Martin's arm and give him a shot of something that almost immediately calmed him to the point where he flopped back into bed and went to sleep. Satisfied with their work, the two orderlies left the room, the lights went out and everything returned to normal.

In the morning Martin looked completely recovered and apparently wasn't going to mention the incident. John asked him if he was alright now.

'How did it look?' Martin asked by way of a reply.

They were having breakfast at the table and Martin was tackling his usual plate of porridge. 'You had some sort of fit,' said John. 'It looked terrible.'

'Nothing to worry about. I used to have real ones when I was drinking. But there's no chance of that in here so I keep them up anyway.'

John put down his piece of toast. 'What are you saying? Do you mean you faked it?'

Martin thought this very funny and was laughing into his plate, decorating his beard with lumps of porridge and milk. 'You've got to give them something to work on, my friend, if you want to get to Broadmoor. What have you given them so far?'

'Well, I've told them about my dreams and drinking the blood of each victim. Does that sound like someone who's sane?'

'Not enough, my vampire. You're expecting them to take your word for it – why should they? They'll look at all your victims and say those were all nicely planned, nice and tidy with the bodies got rid of and everything tidied up afterwards. When you nick their cash and jewellery some genius will say that wasn't for blood but just to make a bob or two. Look at your clothes – nice suit, nice shoes, how are you going to fit into Broadmoor looking like that? When you turn up they'll think you're the new governor,' said Martin, starting to pick the porridge out of his beard.

'What do you suggest, then?' asked John.

'Drink a glass or two of blood here, for breakfast if you like. Start climbing up the walls and say you want to sleep in the rafters.'

John went pale at the prospect. 'I drank my urine once – apparently it's good for something, although I can't remember what right now.'

'That's more like it. But make sure they see you do it. Just don't expect me to use the same glass afterwards,' said Martin, slapping him on the back and asking him for another cigarette.

23

The Reverend Ronald Chalmers was approaching retirement now and helped out with a couple of duty spells at Brixton prison, including a monthly Sunday service that was always well attended, although he believed this was mostly to give the congregation a change of scene rather than any real devotional calling.

As a new arrival, John George Haigh, Prisoner Number 7663, was towards the top of the reverend's visiting list. He found him seated at the table writing a letter. Chalmers introduced himself and asked John if he was comfortable and whether he would like a chat. John said he would and asked if he could see the prison chapel.

As a remand prisoner, there was still a degree of freedom for John, and after Chalmers had checked if he could take John to the chapel 'to pray', the request was granted provided they were accompanied by a warder.

The chapel for John turned out to be surprisingly spacious, with an attractive hammer-beam roof that gave it a feeling that you'd left the prison and now were somewhere different, not holy perhaps but at least a place where you could breathe without clanging doors and people shouting.

'Shall we sit?' asked Chalmers, looking a little nervous of his new charge.

John touched him on the arm. 'Don't worry, I won't bite you,' he said, and things relaxed a little.

They sat in a pew near the front, looking ahead at the altar with its plain cross and two candlesticks without any candles. 'They are removed until a service,' explained Chalmers, 'just in case.'

'You know who I am?' asked John.

'It's difficult not to know who you are after all the fuss in the papers.'

John seemed pleased with this answer. 'You don't mind bringing me in here?'

'In church we are all the same. Do you have a faith?' asked Chalmers.

'I do, of a sort, but there's probably all the difference in the world between yours and mine.'

'Do you want to talk about it?'

'Well, if I have a faith it's a sort of mongrel faith, let me put it like that. My parents were strict Plymouth Brethren. I was their only child, not allowed books except the Bible, no wireless, no magazines and a ten-foot fence around the house to keep out the sins of the world.'

'But you went to school?'

'I went to school but didn't have many friends and just seemed to come home afterwards. Of course there was no chance of inviting anyone home and so that didn't help. But I was musical, could sing and play the piano well and even played the organ at Wakefield Cathedral. They let me trot off to the cathedral at some ungodly hour on Sunday mornings to sing in the choir. My schedule there was acting as server at the altar for communion at six, seven and eight, then the ten-thirty service and Sunday school and finally evening service. I can't think why they let me go because services at Wakefield were very High Church and everything that the Brethren abhorred: Christ skewered on the cross, lots of blood, incense and candles, and us in the choir singing our hearts out. I don't think they had an idea. They saw me as accepting the religious atmosphere with delight at home and happy to be among God's people, as they put it.'

'What effect did all this have on you?'

'It made me a bit cynical. There was this different world that no one had told me about, a world I couldn't really describe to my parents because it would upset them. There was another thing. My father had a blue scar on the top of his head that he told me was because he was a sinner. I asked him why mother hadn't got a scar on her head and he said it was because she was an angel. I was in a panic that I was going to get a blue scar, and every time I committed the smallest of sins I looked in the mirror for a scar, but nothing happened. So I started gearing up the sins and still nothing happened, and in the end decided that I could sin as much as I liked and not have to worry about looking in the mirror.'

Chalmers looked across to John, who sat there looking not the slightest bit sorry for himself, still smiling up at the altar. 'So do you think all this explains the situation you find yourself in now?' said Chalmers, trying to put the question as tactfully as possible.

'Look at it this way. I won a prize for a divinity essay at school and I can remember the last sentence now. "We may well learn the lesson that one fall, even though it be met with perfect grace and full restoration, does not cure a natural disposition, though it may go far to correct it." A little pompous, perhaps, but I believed in the idea of a natural disposition then and I believe it now. I was born with a disposition and nothing was going to change it. My parents believed this as members of the Brethren. If we believed in Christ we wouldn't be judged. Then I started having dreams.'

'What sort of dreams?'

'Dreams that I was walking in a forest of dripping wet trees and that when I got closer I saw they were dripping with blood that was being collected by a figure holding a bowl. When I got near him he held the bowl out to me and told me to drink.'

'You've told your doctors about this?'

'I have told Dr Yellowknees, yes. I think it was the figure of Christ dying on that cross in Wakefield that did it for me. I couldn't say that to my parents, of course – that was my world and I had to keep it that way. I really wanted to help Him and couldn't. I've never wanted to hurt anybody, you know. That probably sounds rather odd coming from me, but I haven't – none of my victims knew anything was going to happen to them and it's always been quick.'

The warder at the back of the chapel left his post at the door to sit in a pew and rest his feet.

'You say you have a faith that might not be very like mine,' asked Chalmers.

'I do, I have a very strong faith. Where we probably differ is that I believe in what I call the Principle, where God commands all we do in life. A natural disposition, if you like – it follows from that if I was marked down to kill from the start of my life then I have to accept this. It's no use worrying about it. It's given me a good life, and if that has to end now then so be it. I shall have to accept it just the way my victims had to accept it. Do as you would be done by, that's a fundamental Christian tenet.'

John sat back in his pew, thinking about what he'd said.

'But the commandments say thou shall not murder, if you don't mind me reminding you,' said Chalmers.

'I killed, but I didn't murder. I had no choice.'

'And took their property.'

'Remember Christ said we should ask the people to supply our daily demands.'

'But you didn't ask – you took.'

'I've made them saints – they gave me everything, their money, their property and their lives.'

'But they gave it to you, not to God.'

'But I am part of God because I do His will. I have no choice in that.'

The Reverend Chalmers wondered where this conversation was going. 'Before we go back to your quarters, would you like to pray?'

John stood up. 'I don't have to pray. I'm part of God, so in that sense I don't have to pray to Him because I'm with Him all the time.'

John sat down again and stared at the altar with its cross and candlesticks. 'You see, I feel more part of God than all this here and you as a priest. Christ did not talk about starting a state or a Church: He wanted all this to be inside us, not outside. For me my conscience is the voice of God. I don't believe He wanted to be worshipped. If you'd made something as wonderful as this world of ours, would you expect to be worshipped? I think I'd be rather embarrassed by people going down on their knees in front of me. Thank you, but I don't want to pray.'

They walked back to John's section of the prison with the warder. They thanked the warder for his patience in accompanying them to the chapel. 'Not at all, sir,' he replied to Chalmers. 'Glad to get a bit of peace and quiet, to be honest – especially sitting there with someone who might meet his Maker before the rest of us.'

As Chalmers said his goodbyes, John thanked him for coming and said he'd like to see him again when he had time. 'You know,' said John. 'I'm either going to end up being made a saint or put in the Chamber of Horrors – either way I shall be a waxwork.'

'I'm sure God will make an appropriate choice,' said Chalmers, and he made his way back out into the rainy streets of Brixton.

24

John was composing his daily letter to Barbara and running short of things to say to her. It was the same with his parents, although he'd added a bonus to each letter today with a poem he'd written for them, entitled 'Silence and Solitude':

> Silence and Solitude, Each lovely word
> Is lovelier for the other. Oh to be
> In some still haunt of their felicity
> A shady hollow where no leaf is stirred
> Whose drowsy stillness mutes the singing bird
> A sunny chamber looking to the sea
> So far removed its rhythmic melody
> Comes back out faintly, rather felt than heard
>
> Silence and Solitude! Beneath their spell
> Old wounds are healed. Sad heats are comforted.
> Eyes find clear vision, and the weary soul
> Once more believes that all may yet be well;
> Feels that its footsteps are divinely led,
> And presses with new vigour towards its goal.

'You look a little down tonight, my poet friend,' said Martin, reading over his shoulder. 'Would you like me to sing for you?'

'No thank you, Martin. It was going into the chapel this afternoon, I think,' John replied. Supper was long finished and most of the prisoners had gone over to their beds to read, smoke or just lie there with their own thoughts. Only Martin and John remained, the former pacing the room with his incessant talk and singing, the latter sitting at the table, writing to Barbara, his parents or notes for his legal team for the next time he met them.

'Did I tell you my dad was a vicar?' asked Martin.

'Many times.'

'He left me alone most of the time, then he'd ask me a question that sent me into spin like what was I going to do with my life and help only comes to those who help themselves. All that sort of crap, you know what I mean?'

'The chapel reminded me of Wakefield and my time as a chorister. I was good at music, Martin, they gave me a scholarship, the only thing I was only ever really good at.'

'You're good at murders, my friend, don't forget.'

'Not that good, otherwise I wouldn't be in here. The reverend told me it was one of the commandments not to murder. I told him if that was God's will then there was nothing I could do about.'

'That's right, that's right.' Martin gave him a pat on the back.

'So to follow from that I shouldn't be tried under these laws if it was all going to happen in the first place.'

'That was the same for me. My friend – well, I thought he was my friend – had it coming to him anyway. He provoked me right over the top.'

'Well, I didn't quite mean it like that, Martin. But thanks anyway. I'm following your advice, by the way.'

'You are?'

'I've shown Dr Matheson how I drink my urine, and I told the reverend about my dreams about the trees dripping blood. Not bad, eh?'

'What about a drink of blood, that would do it. We'll have you in Broadmoor before you can count to six.'

Martin sat down at the table beside his friend. He took the Parker pen out of John's hand. 'Now, that's a nice pen. Do you want me to write to Barbara and tell her what a good bloke you are?'

'I'll have to tell her that's it for us. I can't expect to carry on. These visits are breaking her up.'

'You said you were a bit iffy about the women.'

'They interfere with more serious work, and I've always said lovemaking is an overrated pastime. But Barbara's been a good friend. We've got a lot in common, music and that sort of thing.'

'Nothing more than a friend, you know what I mean? Lovely young girl, there must have been more.'

'Nothing more. I wouldn't have married her, the last experience was bad enough.'

'Were you – you know – going to get rid of her, like the others?' asked Martin, looking straight ahead at the wall.

'Good God, no – she hasn't any money.' said John, the smile coming back to his lips.

'I haven't any money either. I should tell you that, in case you get any ideas.'

'You don't have to worry about that, Martin. Beside, with those shoulders I'd never get you into the pot,' said John, taking his turn to slap Martin on the back.

In his aimless way, Martin had been leafing through a large desk diary of John's that recorded all his visits and letters. When John slapped him on the back, Martin dropped the diary and a couple of signed photos fell out on to the desk. One was of a middle-aged man in a dinner jacket and black tie, taken in a studio, with the studio icon in the bottom left of the picture; the other was of a younger man with a moustache, taken in the street outside what looked like an amusement arcade. The first was signed 'Love, Archie' and the second, 'Always lucky, Your Friend, Mac'.

'Who are these?' asked Martin.

'Oh, friends of mine. This one got me a job when I came to London and the other was a good friend with whom I was doing some business – we were going to manufacture tubular chairs together,' said John, smiling affectionately as he looked from one photo to another.

'What happened to them?'

'I had to get rid of them. We became too friendly, you see. The second one, Archie, had a wife and she was becoming difficult. I had to get rid of her as well,' said John, the smile not faltering.

Martin shifted a few inches along the bench from John. 'That's a lot of people.'

'Six in all with Mac's parents and Mrs Durand-Deacon,' admitted John. 'All lovely people. I think it was Archie's left foot they found in the workroom yard.'

Martin wasn't singing any more. He sucked his teeth and nearly threw up. 'What about the woman, the one you're being tried for?' he asked in a whisper.

John carefully folded the two photographs back into the diary. 'Olive was nice. She was twice my age. She knew more about music than I did. She knew more about everything than I did, but I think I amused her. She was posh and well bred through and through. But I was running out of money. They were all good friends of mine, Martin, but that's the way it had to be otherwise how would I have known exactly how much they were worth and where all the money was? Olive was nearly seventy and so she hadn't much time to enjoy it all and I'm sure she'd have been glad that I was taking it all over.'

'No regrets, then, that you liked your friends and took their money?'

'None at all. I'd do it again. You see, petty crime is okay but it doesn't make much. Then you go to prison for a few years and come out broke and have to do it all again. To get into the big money you have to go the full hog and then you have enough for the next five years or so. My only gripe with Olive was that she carried too much weight and I couldn't get rid of it.'

Martin moved back along the bench towards John. 'But you were going to get caught.'

John took his lovely pen back off Martin before he ruined the nib playing darts on the table. 'Remember the previous five were undetected. I'd committed the perfect murders and that made me lazy. When you think about it I should have carted all the remains of Olive into the countryside, along with Archie's foot, and dumped them there instead of the yard, the drums, the whole lot. I got careless but you do after so many times. I should have gone on picking people I could explain away. With Mac I told his parents he'd disappeared to avoid the draft. With the Hendersons I paid their hotel bill and said they'd moved to South Africa. I didn't have to explain to their dog, I just took him for walks and he was happy. But with Olive half the world started asking where she was.'

Martin picked up the pen again and started unscrewing the top and then screwing it back up again. 'That was hers,' said John.

'What was?' asked Martin.

'That was Olive's pen,' said John. Martin put it back down swiftly.

John took off his glasses and put them down on the table beside the pen. 'And those were Archie's, but at least I changed the lenses.'

'But doesn't that make it all worse, knowing them all so well?'

'Well, you killed your friend.'

'That was different. We were always fighting but I'd never wanted to kill him. We were drunk.'

'I think that shows rather a disregard for your friend, killing him on the spur of the moment. I spent months, if not years, planning mine. I think that shows a respect, don't you think?'

'I think you're mad, my friend, that's what I think. I think they'll have you banged up in Broadmoor in no time and then your pretty Barbara will come and visit you. I might even join you and we can live the life of Riley. They do them pretty well down there, you know.'

John's brow furrowed. 'I think that's where you might be wrong. They're going to say I spent too much time planning all this to be mad. That's the test, my lawyer people tell me, did I know what I was doing was wrong?'

'And if we don't get into Broadmoor?' asked Martin.

'Then we have an appointment with the great Mr Pierrepoint, the man I've always wanted to meet because he's killed more people than I have. Now, isn't that madness?'

Someone in the room told them to go to bed and stop talking, but the night screw hadn't arrived and so Martin told him to shut up himself otherwise he'd come over and sort him out.

'The thing I've always wanted to know,' said Martin, lowering his voice, 'is whether it hurts.'

'What, getting hanged? Of course it doesn't hurt. It breaks the neck, as long as they've calculated the drop properly. Now, that is something I'd want to check with our friend Pierrepoint.'

'I want my dad to be there,' said Martin.

'I thought you said you didn't want anything to do with him.'

'He's a clergyman and knows what to do on these sort of occasions. He hasn't been much use the rest of my life.'

'Well,' replied John, 'I think it should be done in public. What's there to hide? If we've been condemned by the public then we should end it in public. I'd like the chance to make a speech and thank everyone for coming, and tell them nothing I did or they were going to do was going to make any difference.'

'You'd bore them to death,' said Martin.

The night screw arrived and told them to go to bed.

25

A week before the trial another prison psychiatrist, Dr H.K. Snell, the principal medical officer at Wormwood Scrubs prison, examined John. Dr Snell saw John at Brixton for a total interview time of four and a half hours, approximately twice the time that Dr Yellowlees was going to examine John for the defence.

John described how he'd attended Wakefield Grammar School with a choral scholarship until the age of 16 or 17 but had failed his school certificate. Nevertheless, he'd obtained a prize for geography and two for divinity. He said he found his home life 'irksome' and subject to limitations that made him want to get away. He found he had a gift for forgery that was so good he was able to write reports in his school record book in his teacher's writing.

He considered it no disgrace going to prison. In fact he thought we could all learn 'patience and the benediction of solitude' from a spell in prison. Nevertheless, Snell found his patient smart and of good intelligence but vain, conceited and egocentric. He was pleased with himself and his cleverness. He told Dr Snell that sex had not interested him 'for some time'.

One curious relic not referred to in Snell's report tells us more about John's vanity and how he regarded his 'cleverness'. This was a discourse composed by John in 1945 for an imaginary American audience, as if he'd suddenly received a phone call from the president asking him to prepare a paper on the current economic situation, and with due modesty John had sat down and written his speech:

My Lords, Ladies and Gentleman,

President Roosevelt has released a blueprint for the international post-war security organization. The council would concern itself with the peaceful settlement of international disputes and with the prevention of threats to peace. This primary purpose of maintaining peace and security and the creation, through international co-operation, of conditions of stability and well-being, necessary for peaceful and friendly relations, depends entirely upon the psychological approach of the parties involved and of their inherent psychological constitution.

I am asked to talk about the American contribution towards the economic consequences of the peace. As to why, I have not yet been given a satisfactory answer. I am still open to discover why an honours degree in mathematics should endow the most meagre knowledge of economics. And this is why I am going to skirt the subject in as cursory a fashion as possible. The whole question of the peace, no matter what the bright and happy prospects of its present pregnancy might be, is wholly dependent upon the psychological treatment of every nation concerned in its development.

The discourse continues for several thousand words and must have taken some time and effort to write, possibly to coincide with the feeling of importance and achievement of becoming a permanent resident of the Onslow Court Hotel, with a smart car sitting down in the street and a fat bank balance from the sale of the McSwans' properties and assets. At any time the phone might ring and he'd be asked to sort out the world situation.

When Dr Snell examined John as to his motives for killing twice in the cases of the McSwan parents and the Hendersons, he was inconsistent with his answers, on one occasion saying he needed more blood after drinking that of his first victim and on another saying he got such pleasure from the first that he wanted to do it again. He denied the obvious motive of financial gain, saying all the killings were 'unlooked for'.

Instead, he said, providence had intended the whole proceeding, in the form of a principle life force or spirit, at the heart of all being. He believed he had a mission: to bring health to people, to do them a good turn and to relieve suffering or make them drink their own urine to give them good health. This was related to the murders, and as for Mrs Durand-Deacon, he was led by the Spirit Force to obtain a cup of blood, but he knew it was wrong and that he must get rid of the corpse.

However, warned Dr Snell, this story has grown over the weeks and interviews and been elaborated upon. In short, Dr Snell did not accept this story. His view was that John was of sound mind and not suffering from a disease of the mind for the purpose of the M'Naghten Rules. He believed John was fit to plead at the approaching trial at Lewes in that he would understand what was going on in the trial and be in a position to instruct his lawyers.

As ordered by Mr Justice Humphreys, the trial took place at the next Sussex Summer Assizes, starting on Monday, 18 July 1949 in Lewes County Hall as part of the South-Eastern Circuit. With due ceremony, Mr Justice Humphreys arrived that morning just before ten at County Hall, his arrival heralded with a trumpet fanfare. He was dressed in scarlet robes and a wig, and carrying a nosegay of flowers, a tradition which dated back to the days when judges needed to be protected against the stench of the courts and the real prospect of infection from 'the gaol disease' of typhus.

Before him the high sheriff, in a lace-trimmed blue velvet suit, had arrived in a customary fanfare of trumpets to sit next to the judge on the bench; it was his duty to arrange for the attendance of the executioner should the prisoner be sentenced to death.

Underneath all this, in an interview room below the courts, John could hear the fanfare as he sat talking to his counsel and solicitor. He was dressed, despite the heat, in a thick herring-bone suit and green silk tie, white handkerchief folded in his breast pocket and his worsted coat thrown over the chair behind him; a newspaper, given to him by one of the escorting police officers on the way down from Brixton that morning, was open at the crossword on his lap.

The interview room was barely large enough to hold the corpulent figure of Sir David Maxwell Fyfe – who had a pear-shaped body, large square bald head and heavy eyebrows – and his junior barrister and solicitor. Sir David sat at the table, already dressed in his gown and neck tabs but as yet without a wig, smoking a cigarette. He had spent most of the journey down from London discussing where they might have lunch. John now sat opposite him, while junior counsel had the remaining chair and their solicitor was obliged to stand.

'Now, Mr Haigh, I'm not going to be asking the prosecution witnesses many questions this morning because there aren't many questions to ask,' said Maxwell Fyfe. 'The reason for this, as you are aware, is that we are not questioning the veracity of these good people because, to put it in a word, you are guilty as hell.'

John beamed at 'Old Maxy', as he called him. He liked people straight talking, especially ones who had made a name for themselves prosecuting Nazi war criminals, like Sir David and the man who was prosecuting that morning, Sir Hartley Shawcross, the present attorney general. Only three years ago it had been Goering, Hess and Ribbentrop at the centre of their attention, and now it was John George Haigh.

Tomorrow the papers would be full of it.

'No, we keep our powder dry and tomorrow we rely on Dr Yellowlees on the insanity issue,' continued Sir David. 'But it won't be easy, he's not willing to go the whole hog on whether you knew you were doing wrong. But he's all we've got. Anything you want to ask before we go up?'

Sir David threw his cigarette on the floor and ground it out with the heel of his shoe while he waited for an answer. John looked down at his crossword. 'Heavy going for the conductor – anagram of orchestra,' John read out, but neither 'Old Maxy' nor anyone else in the room were in the mood.

'I understand you're writing your life story for the *News of the World* while all this is going on. For God's sake don't let them or anyone else publish it until the trial and any appeal are over. We don't want another run-in with a newspaper, especially if you've written the article,' said Sir David.

'I haven't finished it yet – I thought there would be plenty of time during the trial,' replied John, before his legal team left.

'Juries don't like smart arses,' said Sir David to his colleagues as they climbed the stone stairs back up to the courts.

At 10.30 a.m. sharp John was led up his own flight of steps into the dock, where he emerged like a badger from his sett, blinking at the rows of barristers with solicitors sitting behind them, a packed public gallery and the press box a hive of activity with reporters coming and going and jostling for a good seat. He knew Barbara would be in the gallery somewhere but couldn't bring himself to look. She was there, attentive as usual, in a light-blue dress with pearls around her neck, her light-brown hair in tight curls. Another lady was in a pink dress with roses on a white hat, making the place look more like Ascot than an assize court trying a capital offence.

The sheriff sat in front of the judge on a stage draped in wine-coloured curtains, dressed in all his finery and carrying his ceremonial sword. Clerks scurried in and out of court bringing messages written on small pieces of paper, and the clerk to the court read these while carrying on a conversation with counsel in a bored sort of way.

Not since he was a novice chorister at Wakefield Cathedral had John felt quite such the centre of attention, stuck up at the front with the congregation gazing at him perform a solo. Now he was solo again but with nothing to sing. He'd brought the newspaper with him up into court and started doing the crossword. That would produce the right note: someone with the education and intelligence to do the crossword but not overawed by the situation.

His solicitor leaned over the side of the dock with a kindly word of encouragement, which he'd barely uttered before the clerk asked the court to rise for the entrance of the judge.

Mr Justice Humphreys entered court from a door behind the bench like the weatherman on a cuckoo clock. He was followed by his clerk, who pulled his seat back for him as he bowed to the court, pushed it forward once the judge was seated and then passed him his red notebook, opening it at a fresh page. The face under the wig was lugubrious, bottom lip sticking out like a child who's been refused a sweet, the forehead furrowed and the cheeks pitted by some of the country's most notorious criminal trials.

The prisoner was asked by the clerk of the assize to stand, which he did after carefully removing the newspaper from his lap and putting it on the chair behind him. 'John George Haigh, you stand charged that you, on the eighteenth day of February of this year in this county, murdered Olive Henrietta Helen Olivia Robarts Durand-Deacon. How say you upon this indictment, are you guilty or not guilty?'

John looked up at the judge with the sheriff next to him. 'I plead not guilty,' he said clearly, his voice rather higher than usual.

The clerk asked him to sit and a jury, ten men and two women, was sworn in. No one paid much attention as to who exactly was being selected for the jury. The clerk then informed them that the prisoner had pleaded 'not guilty' and said, 'Your charge is to hearken unto the evidence and say whether he be guilty or not guilty.'

Next Attorney General Sir Hartley Shawcross, KC, MP got to his feet to open for the prosecution. An urbane and composed figure, as good looking as any matinee idol, he had been deadly enough to send half the Nazi hierarchy to the scaffold after the defeat of Germany.

But the image he conjured in his opening was a world away from the atrocities of war and more reminiscent of an Agatha Christie novel. 'May it please your lordship,' he started. 'Members of the jury, in February of this year there had been residing for some time in a quiet Kensington hotel the two persons with whom you will be mainly concerned in this case. The first of those persons was the prisoner, a man apparently without any regular source of income, who, at the material time, was in debt, withdrawn at the bank to the extent of about £80 and being pressed for the payment of his hotel bill. The second of those persons was a Mrs Durand-Deacon, a lady of comfortable circumstances, living peacefully there in the evening of her life.'

Oh, Olive would like that, thought John. It was one thing being shot in the head and bundled into a vat of sulphuric acid but being described as a person 'in the evening of her life' at the age of 69 was beyond the pale. Alright, she had nearly thirty years on him, but she'd told him about her militant days as a suffragette and throwing a brick through a window that earned her a night in the police cells. In some ways she had been the perfect mother to him, the mother he never had; she had wanted to take him into the world of art and politics, not shut him up like a prisoner behind 10ft walls.

'Members of the jury, I shall put this case before you as one which, although it is attended by unpleasant, sordid, and even nauseating features, is in reality an exceedingly simple case of a carefully maintained murder for gain,' continued the attorney general. 'In this connection there is no such thing as a nice murder or a nasty murder.'

He's right there, of course, thought John, making another note. Murder is beyond right and wrong, beyond nice or nasty, it's simply moving money around from one account to another.

The attorney general recited the facts of the murders and the subsequent selling of Mrs Durand-Deacon's jewellery much as John had told the police. However, he paused at the moment when the detective inspector left the interview room at Chelsea Police Station for a few minutes and John had turned to Inspector Webb and asked what his chances were of being released from Broadmoor.

'Members of the jury,' Sir Hartley continued. 'Broadmoor, as I daresay you have heard, is a criminal lunatic asylum in which those who are found guilty of crimes but are insane at the time, may be detained; you may think that was a curious enquiry for the prisoner to make at that time. It is a matter for you, and you will consider it in its context as the case develops. There was certainly no sign, then, of reason tottering upon its throne but rather, you may think, an indication of careful premeditation in the prisoner's mind about the lines on which he must meet the charge which, as he must have known at that time, was likely to be made against him.

'The prisoner asserts in his statement that, having killed this unfortunate woman, he proceeded to drink some of her blood. Members of the jury, that statement may or may not be true and may or may not be relevant, but you will remember that previously he had made this enquiry about the chances of being released from Broadmoor.

'When a man, apparently sane, is charged with murder to which there is no kind of answer, no possible answer on the facts, before he can look forward to getting out of Broadmoor he has to consider how he can get himself in. At any rate, whether you are satisfied that the prisoner had this morbid appetite for blood or not, you may think that it does nothing to detract from what the prosecution suggest was the primary motive for this murder, namely, financial gain.'

In the end the attorney general was on his feet for an hour and a half in delivering his opening speech and, on this warm summer's day, was then glad to sit down, have a sip of water and let his junior counsel start the examination of the prosecution witnesses.

26

The prosecution witness whom John Haigh least wanted to see was probably his former business partner Edward Jones, and the sensitivity of his evidence was marked by the attorney general himself rising to examine him after several less important witnesses had been dealt with by his junior counsel.

Edward Charles Rowland Jones was called by the ushers from the corridor outside, and in his walk from the courtroom door to the witness box he looked more like a prisoner than a witness. His shoulders drooped, and he seemed to have aged ten years with the revelation that his partner and friend for the last four years had not only killed six people in that time but disposed of half of them on his business premises too.

Jones explained that he'd offered John Haigh a directorship in the company and, although John said he'd like the opportunity, the matter was dropped. Instead he had been their unpaid business representative in London on a friendship basis. In return John was allowed to use the storeroom at Leopold Road. On some occasions he would use it without asking, and on one occasion Jones asked him what he was doing and John replied it was 'a conversion job' without giving any more detail.

Jones explained to the court how on the morning of Friday 18 February he met John at the Leopold Road premises and shifted some steel pieces from there to the main factory in West Street. John said he might be bringing someone down to the factory to discuss the manufacture of artificial fingernails. He came to the West Street factory at about quarter to five to say they hadn't turned up.

During the course of the following week John managed to pay only £36 of the £50 he owed him, and then on the Tuesday afternoon the police arrived.

'On the following day, Wednesday the twenty-third, did you see the prisoner again?' asked Sir Hartley.

'Yes,' replied Jones. 'He came in just before lunchtime. I told him I had been interviewed by the police, and I asked him if he'd been up to anything. I said I hoped he was not in any trouble. He shrugged his shoulders and said "No" and just laughed. Prior to his leaving, I said to him, "If there is any trouble, I prefer you not to come to the works; I prefer you to stay away if there is any trouble." He shrugged his shoulders and then laughed; he offered no reply to my suggestion then.'

For the first time Edward Jones now looked over to the dock as if his friend might, even at this late stage, say sorry, or even repay the £14 he still owed him, but the prisoner was looking down at the newspaper on his lap, pen in hand, doing the crossword.

'When you finally entered the storeroom with the police did you see a rubber apron, rubber gloves and a gas-mask case?' continued Sir Hartley

'Yes.'

'Did those things belong to you?'

'No, they were on the premises, but they were not my property.'

'Had you seen them before?'

'No.'

Mr Justice Humphreys was asked if he wanted to ask the witness any questions after Maxwell Fyfe had declined the offer. The judge thought a moment, perhaps seeing the witness look over to the dock, and asked, 'Did you notice anything peculiar about Haigh at all on these days between the fifteenth of February and the last time you saw him?' he asked.

'Nothing unusual,' Jones replied.

'You saw nothing unusual at all about him?'

'No,' repeated Jones, without even having to think about it.

While Edward Jones was the only witness who could be remotely described as a friend of John's, Constance Lane was probably the only real friend of Olive's to be called to give evidence, apart from Mrs Birin of the Francis Bacon Society, who confirmed she'd had lunch with Olive when the fingernails were discussed with John. A diminutive figure dressed in black, Constance Lane now stepped up to the witness box, where she nearly disappeared inside the stand.

Sir Hartley also reserved this witness for himself, asking if she'd prefer to sit and thankful that she refused as he'd probably lose sight of her altogether. 'Do you live at the Onslow Court Hotel, Kensington?' he asked.

'Yes, I have been living there for about nine years,' came the firm reply.

'Was Mrs Durand-Deacon one of your friends at the hotel?'

'A great friend.'

'Did you see her on Friday the eighteenth of February?'

'Yes, at about 2.15.'

'Did you have a talk with her?'

'Yes.'

'Was she a lady who was particular about her appearance?'

'Very particular.'

'Did she wear jewellery or not?'

'Yes, on and off she did.'

'You saw her at 2.15 on that day; was her table unoccupied that night at dinner?'

'Yes.'

'On the following morning did you have a conversation with Mr Haigh?'

'I did.'

'You knew him as another resident in the hotel?'

Mrs Lane took her first look at the dock, where John had stopped gazing at the crossword and was now looking across the court at her, smiling slightly and poking the end of his pen into his mouth as if considering making a note. 'As a nodding acquaintance only,' she said tersely and looked back at counsel.

She went on to describe how John had driven her to Chelsea Police Station, at his suggestion, to report Olive's disappearance, make their statements and then how he drove her back to the hotel. 'That is the last conversation I had with Mr Haigh,' she concluded.

At this point Mr Justice Humphreys interrupted. 'Had he a car of his own?' he asked.

'I think so,' said Mrs Lane. 'At least he drove the car,' she agreed, as if John might have pinched that as well.

Sir Hartley produced the remains of a handbag, heavily stained and with the handle missing, although not too discoloured to see that it was red.

'Have you seen that handbag before?' he asked.

The handbag was brought over to Mrs Lane by an usher for closer inspection. 'Yes, I have. It is Mrs Durand-Deacon's handbag.'

'When you saw her on the Friday had she got the handbag with her?'

'Yes.'

'Was it that handbag?'

'Yes.'

The judge interrupted for a second time. 'Where was that handbag found?' he asked.

'It was found in the sludge at the yard at Leopold Road, my lord,' replied Sir Hartley.

There was a silence in court for a moment. It was as if the full import of the horror of what they were all talking about that morning came home after the glib technical talk earlier of rubber gloves, quantities of acid and drums. The handbag was nearly the only thing to accompany its owner through her murder, her cremation in acid until she was dumped as sludge in the yard and now her trial.

Nearly the only thing, but not quite.

27

In most murder cases there is a body for the pathologist to examine and identify a cause and time of death, along with incidental details such as when the deceased last ate and other matters that might be vital in discovering the murderer. When there is no body then the pathologist can help in finding it and then identifying whose body it is as well as their sex and age.

John Haigh had made so few mistakes in disposing of his first five victims that had he not chosen Mrs Durand-Deacon as number six then the chances are that he might have got away with it; her disappearance caused too many questions to be asked and this, inevitably, is what led to his arrest. The circumstantial evidence was overwhelming, but there was still no body, and pathologist Dr Keith Simpson was brought in to see if John was telling the truth when he said he had dissolved the body in sulphuric acid and tipped the remains into the yard outside the storeroom.

However, one mistake John had made was his misinterpretation of the legal principle of *corpus delicti* to mean that if there was no body then there could be no charge of murder. In the days of his workroom in the basement at Gloucester Road, the bodies of his first three victims could be completely disposed of through the drain, and even if body parts had not completely dissolved there was little chance of them being discovered, let alone traced to a victim or murderer.

But in Leopold Road there was no such convenient drain, and the sludge and remains of anything that had failed to dissolve lay exactly where John had said it would be in his confession: the storeroom yard.

Dr Keith Simpson was now sworn in and gave his address as Harley Street, London, and his profession as pathologist at Guy's Hospital. He was a slightly built man in a double-breasted suit, carrying a black hombre hat that he placed on the side of the witness stand, opening a file and balancing that in front of him as if he was about to deliver a lecture.

He told the court how on entering the storeroom with the police they found a group of finely scattered bloodstains under the windows and that he'd taken extensive areas of soil from the yard for sifting and examination. In the soil he'd found the handle of a red plastic handbag, a lipstick-container cap and intact full upper and lower dentures. He had also found various human remains, including some gallstones and a number of body parts, which enabled him to conclude they were part of one body that had been dissolved in sulphuric acid, that of an older woman. 'I formed the view that if a person standing at that bench between the windows were shot through the head from behind, that might account for the blood splashes I saw on the wall,' he added. 'If a pad of cotton wool were used that would limit the flow of blood from the entry and exit holes of the bullet.'

Chief Inspector Guy Mahon gave evidence that he'd accompanied Keith Simpson to Leopold Road and found two pieces of red cellophane on the bench and a hairpin at the bottom of the green drum. Later he'd found a blue shirt with blood on the cuffs in the prisoner's hotel room and a brown-handled penknife with traces of blood on the blades and shaft in the glovebox of the Alvis.

'Did the prisoner tell you about this penknife?' the attorney general asked.

'Yes,' replied Mahon.

'Did he say what it had been used for?'

'Not exactly that knife. He told me the penknife he had used to tap Mrs Durand-Deacon for blood was in his car.'

'Where did you find that penknife, in fact?'

'I found it in the cubbyhole of the dashboard of that motor car. He did say, "I do not think that is the knife: I think the knife had a yellow handle".'

'That was the only knife you could find in his car?'

'Yes, I searched the car thoroughly again, and I found no other knife.'

Dr Holden, Director of the Metropolitan Police Laboratory at New Scotland Yard, and his deputy director, Dr Turfitt, concluded the forensic evidence. Dr Holden said that he found both sleeves and the bottom of the fur coat were patched and matched the pieces of fabric found in a sewing bag in Mrs Durand-Deacon's room at the hotel. He also found human bloodstains on the rubber apron, mixed with odd fibres of beech wood, suggesting that the wooden rod had been wiped on the apron after being used to stir the acid and body. The recovered handbag had been immersed in acid, rotting the stitches and falling to pieces. There were only the merest traces of blood on the penknife.

Dr Turfitt had examined the revolver in its holster and confirmed it had been used recently. The judge interrupted to ask whether it was an English revolver and was told it was Dr Henderson's Enfield revolver. Dr Turfitt also examined the half gallstone found in the earth in the yard and confirmed it was a typical human type gallstone of the soft cholesterol type.

Finally the attorney general turned to Exhibit 40, the stirrup pump. 'Has this been corroded, both inside and out, by sulphuric acid?' he asked, and as he did so he picked up the pump, only to drop it as if it had bitten him, his fingers burnt by remains of the acid on the base of the pump. John looked up from his crossword as the pump clattered back on to the table and started to giggle, putting his hand up to his mouth to control himself.

As usual Sir David Maxwell Fyfe had no questions. The attorney general said that concluded the case for the Crown and sat down, nursing his hands.

28

The trial so far to the uninitiated seemed strangely one-sided, with the prosecution calling or reading out the statements of over thirty witnesses and the defence hardly bothering to say anything in response, let alone challenge the witnesses in any dramatic cross-examinations. The evidence seemed so overwhelming and so horrific it might have been kinder to let John Haigh plead guilty and be done with it. Aware of this, Sir David Maxwell Fyfe now got to his feet to do some explaining.

Sir David was a big man, wrapping his gown around him and flapping the tail of his wig like an overweight penguin. He spoke more slowly than Sir Hartley, always giving himself time to rehearse what he was about to say, refusing to be rushed and aware he had one witness and one witness only to rely on to save his client going to the gallows.

'Members of the jury, as you have heard from an intimation which my lord allowed me to make earlier, the defence in this case is concerned and depends on the state of the mind of the accused man. Therefore, I am sure you will not misunderstand or hold against the defence that they have taken what appears to be a somewhat passive part in that part of the case which deals with the facts of the killing,' he said apologetically.

'It is now, as I see it, the proper time for me to explain to you the evidence which will be put before you to show that the accused man was insane at the time of committing the act charged against him so as not to be responsible in law for what he did. The course that I have taken of not dealing with the actual facts and particulars of the killing here corresponds with the special verdict for which I am going to ask you, which is in the form of guilty of the act charged, but insane at the time when it was committed,' said Sir David.

Ah, so that was it, the vampire was going to try to say he was mad and get off scot-free. The jury was now going to be asked to earn their keep after the entertainment of the prosecution evidence. Well, he could try. Sir David felt like a schoolmaster who'd let his class watch a horror film, and then put them into detention rather than let them go home. He watched the eyes of his class of twelve start to glaze.

'Members of the jury, may I say one other preliminary word to you, because this is a difficult issue to put in a way which is most helpful to you in order that you may understand it,' he warned, tactfully explaining that he would simplify what he was about to say, but they probably wouldn't understand it anyway.

'But may I put it in this way: every man is presumed to be sane and to possess a sufficient degree of reason to be responsible for his crimes until the contrary is proved to the satisfaction of the jury. The second point is that the accused was labouring under a defect of reason, and that such defect of reason arose from a disease of the mind; and thirdly that the accused did not know the nature and quality of his act or, if he did, he didn't know he was doing wrong.'

Sir David was here outlining for the jury the M'Naghten Rules, devised by the House of Lords in 1843 when one Daniel M'Naghten had shot and killed the prime minister's secretary believing he was the prime minister. M'Naghten was sufficiently paranoid to believe the whole world was against him, including Prime Minister Sir Robert Peel, and he had travelled down from Scotland with the aim of murdering him. By the time he reached Downing Street he was ready to shoot the first person who emerged from No. 10, which he did.

The difficulty for the court when trying M'Naghten was this: although the man was clearly mad there were no existing rules to define what amounted to insanity sufficient to excuse responsibility and send the accused off to a mental institution for treatment, out of harm's way. The M'Naghten Rules proved so effective that they are still used today, and while they look straightforward they produce two formidable obstacles for a defence team. The first is to show, usually with the help of a psychiatrist giving expert evidence, that the accused does actually suffer from a disease of the mind and not, for example, a bad temper or a grudge against someone, however justified, or a jealous nature. The second is to show that, even if the accused is suffering from a disease of the mind, he or she knew what they were doing was legally wrong.

What the jury did not know in the Haigh case is that a number of doctors, both outside consultants brought in to assess John's mental state as well as internal prison doctors, did not consider him to be insane.

Sir David said he'd been struggling to think of an explanation of the word 'reason' that was not technical and that it was so easy to drop into the jargon of the philosopher and psychologist. Instead he dropped into the jargon of the lawyer. 'It has been well portrayed by one of the greatest advocates who ever graced the English Bar, in the form of something sitting on the throne of the mind, ruling the mentality and able to make the decisions I have mentioned.'

The advocate gracing the English Bar was Lord Erskine (1750–1823), and if Sir David had not yet confused the jury he certainly had now by asking them to define reason as 'something sitting on the thrones of their mind'.

'That brings me to the facts of the case,' said Sir David, coming back down to earth, 'and the disorder of the mind, which I submit has affected the reason of the accused, as that rare but quite well-known type of mental aberration which is called, in psychological medicine, pure paranoia.'

Now paranoia was a condition the jury were aware of in a day-to-day context, from paranoid mothers-in-law to fighting a world war against a man who was racially paranoid. All they needed now was for counsel and his witness to make it more complicated.

'I am going to call Dr Yellowlees, who will give you a full description of that disorder, but I am going to develop the matter with you myself for a few moments. The ordinary dictionary definition is chronic mental unsoundness marked by delusions. Paranoia means a complete and permanent alteration of the entire personality which overwhelms the mental outlook, the character and the conduct of the victim. It is the result of the patient's interests and energies being turned in upon himself and withdrawn from the real world around him from an early stage in his existence. As it develops and gets a greater hold, it amounts practically to self-worship and a conviction that he is in some mystic way under the control of a guiding spirit that means infinitely more to him and is an infinitely greater authority than any human laws or rules of society. He knows that his secret life of fancy has got to be lived alongside the ordinary life of the world and so he's lucid, astute and shrewd when he is not actually acting under the influence of his fantasy,' explained Sir David, suddenly becoming lucid with a clear, almost masterly account of paranoia.

At this point the accused himself was listening carefully to his counsel and wondering how the accounts of his dreams he'd given to the doctors accorded to this definition of paranoia. Not bad, he thought, not bad. As if reading his mind, Sir David proceeded to put his thoughts into words, at the same time keeping an eye on the court clock, aware there was another half hour before the court rose for the day at four o'clock and Dr Yellowlees was not in court as he'd been told he wouldn't be needed until the next day.

'In this case you have these dreams occurring not only in the immediate past but from an early stage in life, with a boy brought up in the most severest surroundings – his parents were extremely severe members of that religious sect known as the Plymouth Brethren – and suddenly changing from that to Wakefield Cathedral, which at that time was extremely High Church. There started in the mind these dreams, which were the result of and which were based on a representation of the bleeding Christ, with the blood dripping from his wounds. From an early age, from about the end of his school time, he believed that he was under a divine guidance and was required to drink his own urine, because of a reading of certain passages that occur in the Bible,' said Sir David, pausing to take a sip of water.

Couldn't have put it better myself, thought John, and wished Martin could be there to hear all this himself: the dreams, the drinking of urine, all wrapped up in a paranoia package that left him, John Haigh, looking and acting quite normal. But what was the jury making of all this? He gave them one last stare for the afternoon, looking for a sign, a nod of the head, a smile of disbelief, but they looked back at him from the other side of the court with an inscrutable, vacant stare.

The jury had, in the course of a long hot day, listened to the evidence of thirty-three witnesses and now, this afternoon, a long, exhausting opening speech that varied from the apologetic to the patronising, from the downright obscure to lucid moments of revelation. And all the time the jury, trying to stay awake and concentrate on what these opposing barristers were saying, were occasionally shifting their gaze to the man in the dock dressed like a city gent, jotting notes that he handed to his solicitor and nearly always smiling, not in a mad way but in a knowing way. He looked a picture of urbane normality, the sort of person they'd like as a bank manager or stockbroker. They'd lost track of the number of people he'd killed. They'd lost track of what Sir David was trying to say about his client being mad. It was hot, and these barristers seemed to have the capacity to go on all day.

At last it was four o'clock. The judge gave them another lecture, this time about not speaking to anyone about what they had heard during the day and, grabbing his red leather notebook, he retreated into his lair for the night.

29

After the lengthy introduction on the previous day by Sir David Maxwell Fyfe, the new day started with the principal defence witness himself, Dr Henry Yellowlees. Sir David read out a long list of the doctor's qualifications, to include fellow of various universities in Scotland and physician and lecturer at St Thomas's Hospital in London for nearly twenty years. He'd also been consulting psychiatrist to the British Expeditionary Force in France in the war, something that carried an unfortunate portent of doom in this early stage of the defence case.

'Doctor of medicine is enough for me,' the judge muttered at the end of this recital of the doctor's qualifications.

Dr Yellowlees cut an austere figure in a dark suit and waistcoat, a man who had put childish things aside, still had the trace of a Scottish accent despite his years in London. He was relishing the opportunity to teach his English colleagues a thing or two about paranoia after they'd all considered John Haigh to be sane, and for this reason knew he had a fight on his hands. From the start he felt a hostility in the court towards him, as if everyone was punch drunk from the horrors they'd heard on the previous day and didn't need doctors today telling them it wasn't his fault.

Dr Yellowlees told the court he'd seen the prisoner in Brixton prison five times, as well as reading all the statements and other documents in the case, and received full co-operation from the prison doctors. 'The first impression I gained of his mental state was that it was obvious that he had what is generally called a paranoid constitution. I had no doubt about that after my first interview with him,' he started. 'This is generally held to result partly from hereditary and partly, or perhaps even more so, from environment, by which I mean specially the early upbringing, the home surroundings and early experiences. Let us take the home conditions, and first of all the religious atmosphere.'

But he'd hardly got the words out when he was interrupted by the judge. 'Before you go any further, will you tell me what you are speaking about? Are we going to have somebody from his home to prove the conditions under which he lived?' he asked.

Sir David hurriedly got to his feet, flapping his wings. 'No, my lord.'

'Then what are you telling me?' asked the judge, and turned to the witness. 'Have you interviewed people at his home?'

Dr Yellowlees did not enjoy being interrupted. 'No,' he replied tersely. 'I said on the facts and statements shown to me on his history.'

'Do you mean what he says about himself or what other people say about him?'

'Both, my lord.'

'We cannot have what other people say about him; that is second-hand evidence. You can tell us what he says about himself, but we cannot have what somebody else is supposed to have said about him.'

'It is not a medical question, my lord,' replied Yellowlees, in effect saying 'sort it out with the lawyers'.

'I agree. I do not understand, Sir David, what you are asking him about.'

'It can be dealt with best on the history he gave himself,' said Sir David, aware of the risk of relying on the word of a serial killer.

'Yes, certainly; what he says himself is evidence,' replied the judge.

Dr Yellowlees continued his evidence, avoiding the eye of the judge and the risk of further interruption. 'He was brought up in a fanatical religious atmosphere and told me that newspapers and radio were both forbidden in his parents' house, that friends and neighbours were excluded and that the wrath and vengeance of God was over his head for every trifling misdemeanour. He also told me that his mother was greatly given to studying dreams, in a fortune-telling or future-telling sense, and believed that the future could be told by them, and he told me that books upon those subjects were very readily available to him, although newspapers and wireless were not.'

'Did he tell you that he used to be a member of the Plymouth Brethren when he was quite young and then joined, in some form or other, Wakefield Cathedral?' asked the judge.

'No, my lord. The only thing he said to me was he never believed in it.'

'Thank you – please continue.'

'If you have a youth with inherited nervous instability, brought up in a solitary atmosphere and with the fear that the unseen and punishing powers are all around him, he tends to run away from them in the only way he can – namely, into a world, in the first place, of fantasy and fairy tale; he will not face his difficulties fairly, and he becomes progressively less able to do so. At first he thinks merely of some clever way of avoiding punishment and, if it develops further and there is no clever way round, he goes into himself, into a world of fantasy and makes an imaginary solution for himself and comes to believe in it.'

Sir David then turned to the religious aspect of the story and asked Dr Yellowlees whether he attached much importance to this. 'Yes, great importance,' he replied. 'Here was this boy or youth in a system or form of worship and belief in which he himself did not believe and of which he was frightened, and then he is plunged into the opposite extreme and a form of worship where ritual and mysticism held a very much more prominent place. By entering into that atmosphere he avoids the conflict between the beliefs which he entertained in his early religion and his developing mind which in a normal person would reject it.'

'Did he give you an account of the dreams that used to trouble him at that time between the ages of ten and sixteen, after he had gone to Wakefield Cathedral?'

'He said that between the ages of ten and sixteen was the period when he was a choirboy and assistant organist and about that time he experienced a constantly recurring dream, which he called the dream of the Bleeding Christ. In this dream, he said, he could see either the head or the whole body of Christ on the cross with blood pouring from His wounds. All along it was the question of blood that was troubling him, and he did say that at that time he could not understand why he had been told that Christ was left to die slowly upon the Cross and was not killed at once.

'The point at which a paranoid constitution develops into a paranoia is when the patient's fantasy world becomes really his psychological home, because it becomes more real to him than his real world, and his fantastic solutions and his ideas of personal cleverness pass all bounds and he regards himself, as nearly as possible, omnipotent. All his other activities, his work, his sexual activities and so forth, are ignored, and the energy which ought to go into them is turned into building up his fantastic life.'

Sir David picked up the point of sexual activity. 'There is one point I just want you to deal with in order to put it aside, but its exclusion is important, I believe. Is there a complete absence of any sex element in the accused's conduct?' he asked.

'Yes, there is a complete absence of any sexual activity or interest, and that in itself, of course, is an abnormal thing.'

'This is not a case where you are depending on the sort of Viennese psychology that everything is related to sex?'

'No, it has nothing to do with that.'

'What is the importance you attach to the absence of sex?'

'It is an indication of a very great abnormality of some kind, that a physically healthy young man, who does not seem to be at all scrupulous in what he does, should have no interest in sex and sexual activity. It happens also to be stated in authoritative works that this is a thing you find in a paranoiac, who sublimates his sexual energies into this worship of himself and his mystic fantasy.'

John looked down at the court from the dock. These men were talking about his sex life, or apparent lack of it, in open court – the cheek of it. If they knew the first thing about his sex life he'd be back in court on another charge and that was another good reason he had to get rid of Mac and Archie. Mac was the easy one, he had no women hanging around him and their relationship grew naturally as they ran the business together. Mac's housemates weren't so lucky – up for gross indecency and importuning males.

Archie was more difficult, he was married and Rose was protective about him and tried to keep John at arm's length. But it was no good and the marriage was under pressure when John broke it up for them.

Even in the middle of court like this John couldn't help seeing the comical side. His parents had chosen to ignore the fact that he'd killed six people and kept up a loving and forgiving correspondence as dutiful parents to a dutiful son, fallen from God's grace as his father put it, but if they'd had a whiff about what was going on in his personal life then they would have been less forgiving. The best thing he did was marry Betty Hamer back in 1934, even though it was a short-lived disaster, because he'd always now be a married man in their eyes.

30

M ost of Dr Yellowlees' evidence so far covered John Haigh's early home life and the problems presented by his moving from the restrictions of the Plymouth Brethren to the High Church atmosphere of Wakefield Cathedral and how all this impacted on the sensitivities of a teenage choirboy. Sooner or later Dr Yellowlees was going to have to say why this should have produced a fraudster and serial killer.

Sir David Maxwell Fyfe now steered his witness into these troubled waters. 'The next point I want you to deal with is what difference did the accused make between these killings and merely the dishonesty of getting other people's goods?' he asked in a business-like manner.

'He was quite clear about that,' replied Dr Yellowlees, to everyone's relief. 'May I go into his previous convictions?'

'Yes,' replied Sir David reluctantly, as if to say 'if you have to'.

'Of his previous convictions he said that the third one was not proper, but the first two he admits, and he says he has to live like anyone else, having good enough wits and rather better than his neighbours, he has to do the best he can, and he really does it to get the artist's joy in doing a good job.'

This declaration of artistic war on the unsuspecting public woke the jury with a jolt. What was all this? No one had mentioned previous convictions.

Dr Yellowlees rubbed it in for them. 'He says that he is like an artist painting a picture, when he has successfully diddled or hoodwinked his fellow creatures.'

Well, thank you, Mr Haigh, thought the jury, the majority of whom had little time for artists anyway, let alone criminal artists.

Dr Yellowlees tried to excuse his patient's behaviour. 'That, of course, is typical of the early paranoid constitution, and shows the conceit and fantasy of it, just as you see in the petty trickster.'

'Are these previous convictions you are talking about convictions for dishonesty?' asked Mr Justice Humphreys.

'Yes, my lord,' said Sir David.

'Not for killing people or for any form of violence?'

'No, not for any form of violence. I am most grateful to your lordship for putting that question,' replied Sir David, without offering to give any more details. He then turned back to Dr Yellowlees. 'I want you to make a distinction between those convictions for dishonesty and these killings.'

'The killings are entirely different, according to his statement,' assured Dr Yellowlees. 'He objects very much to the word "murder", and I think it was almost the only sign of touchiness which he showed; but he does not mind them being called "killings". He has made several statements about it. He said to me he had no special interest in rights and wrongs, or in the laws of the country, or in his victims, because he says this is destiny. He says he has a destiny to fulfil. He believes the killings are the third revelation. He is not quite clear yet but thinks that may have to do with the question of eternal life, but he does not know how.'

The jury began to fade again at the mention of destiny and eternal life. Counsel tried to bring things back to reality by asking if this was related to the outside power he'd mentioned.

'He says he is just an instrument of the outside power. He states that before the killings he had no broad or particular plan; in one case he said that he did not know until a minute or two beforehand that he was going to kill the victim. On the other hand, he states that after the killing he took every precaution to avoid detection, because he knew perfectly well that murder is punishable by law and, like any practical man, he was anxious to avoid it.'

'So he made that distinction between his mental state before and after the crime?'

'Yes,' said Dr Yellowlees.

The lawyers in court started to admire the strategy here. It was one thing to show you were suffering from some mental disease, relying on the technical expertise of the witness, but another to anticipate how the defence was going to get around the next stage of showing that the accused didn't know he was doing something legally wrong, when a feature of this case were the extraordinary lengths he'd gone to in order to cover up the killings. What Haigh seemed to be saying that he was he mad up to and during the killing but recovered sufficiently afterwards to cover up what he'd done because he now knew it was wrong.

Mr Justice Humphreys saw what was going on and interrupted. 'He told you that he took steps to avoid detection afterwards because he knew quite well that to kill a person was a crime?' he asked.

'Yes, I think he used the phrase "punishable by law".'

'Very well, because he knew that to kill a person was punishable by law?'

'Yes, and he added that of course it did not apply in his case.'

'What did not apply in his case?'

'What I have just said, that murder being punishable by law did not apply to him.'

'Does that suggest that he is not amenable to the law?'

'Yes, certainly.'

'Why was he not amenable to the law?'

'Because he says he is working under the guidance and in harmony with some vital principle that is above the law.'

'And, because he said that,' asked the judge, 'he thought that everybody else would believe it – is that what he told you?'

'I would not say that, my lord. The one thing he is not is a malingerer.'

'Does he appear to believe it?'

'Yes, absolutely.'

'He thinks that he ought not to be punished?'

'Yes.'

'Does he really think he will not be punished? Does he think that if he is caught stealing or killing he will not be punished?'

'I asked him that and he said, I am awaiting the trial with complete equanimity; I am in the position of Jesus Christ before Pontius Pilate, and the only thing I have to say, if I was to say anything, would be, He can have no power against me, unless it be given to him from above.'

There was a short silence while the judge considered this. Then he stuck out his lower lip and gave a petulant smile. 'That might well be,' he muttered.

Counsel now wanted to get Dr Yellowlees's evidence wound up. While they still had the judge with them, they had probably lost the jury. Sir David asked the doctor what he made of John Haigh's indifference to his crimes. Dr

Yellowlees said that the absolutely callous, cheerful, bland and almost friendly indifference to the crimes, which he freely admitted to have committed, was unique in his experience. As to the tree dream, Haigh might have been exaggerating the effect it had on him but Dr Yellowlees did not believe it had been invented. As to the drinking of blood, Dr Yellowlees did not think this important from a medical point of view because to a paranoiac it does not matter whether he does things in his imagination or in fact.

Finally Sir David reached the sticking point in Dr Yellowlees's evidence. 'Taking the last question of the legal test, would it be right to say at once that you are not prepared to express an opinion on whether he knew he was doing what was wrong?'

'That is so,' replied Dr Yellowlees slowly.

'In your view what amount of contact with the accused and what opportunities of observation would be necessary in order to make an attempt to answer that question?'

'I don't not think any psychiatrist could answer, or even attempt to answer, that question unless he had lived with such a paranoid patient for years. In other words, your view would be as good as anybody's.'

Mr Justice Humphreys stirred uneasily in his seat. Surely he hadn't sat through all this to have an expert come to court just to say his guess was good as anybody's. 'And, therefore, you prefer to give no answer to that question?' he asked emphatically.

'Yes, I prefer to give no answer to that question.'

Sir David gave his judge a resigned look that said that was the best they could do for the moment and sat down for the prosecution to start their cross-examination, bowing his head slightly to avoid the shells about to whistle over the parapet.

31

Usually at the start of a cross-examination in a murder trial, counsel for the prosecution has to face the accused and a string of defence witnesses to dispute the facts of the case, who did what and where, followed by any medical evidence to look at the accused's state of mind at the time of the crime.

In this case the court had seen a lot of witnesses for the prosecution with little or nothing coming from the defence in cross-examination. Now it was the turn of the defence, which produced only one witness, a doctor who was willing to give a long lecture on paranoia. This doctor then said nothing about the accused's perception of right and wrong, except that when he had done something wrong he enjoyed a lucid interval that allowed him to cover his tracks and that if he could distinguish right from wrong then he considered himself above the law anyway, as he was guided by some higher force.

Sir Hartley Shawcross, who only four years ago headed the British prosecution of the Nazis at Nuremberg, now got to his feet to do battle with Dr Yellowlees. If the Nazis had excelled at anything besides genocide it was bureaucracy, and Sir Hartley now seemed to want to show that the doctor couldn't even keep his numbers and dates organised.

'You said when you gave your evidence that you had seen the prisoner five times, you had examined him five times. That is not accurate, is it?' he asked with his first question.

Dr Yellowlees looked slightly startled at the question. 'I believe it to be accurate or I should not have said so,' he replied tersely.

'Look at your notes,' said Sir Hartley, taking over the schoolmaster role. 'When did you see him first?'

Dr Yellowlees looked bleakly at his folder of notes. 'I really do not know the dates – between the first and sixth of July.'

'Would you accept it from me that the first time you saw the prisoner was on the first of July?'

'Yes.'

'For twenty-five minutes?'

'I dare say.'

'The second time on the second of July for forty-five minutes, and the third time on the fifth of July for forty-five minutes. You visited Brixton prison on two other occasions and discussed the case with Dr Matheson, but you didn't see the prisoner?'

'I did not think that is quite right. I am prepared to accept it and I am sorry if I made a mistake.'

'I must put it to you that you saw the prisoner in all for two hours and ten minutes, forty minutes longer than your evidence has so far taken. Is that right?'

'I have got no idea,' replied Dr Yellowlees, unsure whether this was a criticism of his being long-winded in giving his evidence or whether he should have seen the patient for longer. But the ticking-off wasn't finished.

'Let us see if we can agree about this,' continued the attorney general. 'You would agree, would you not, that the prisoner is a person on whose word it would be utterly unsafe to rely?'

'Yes.'

'But you have, as a matter of fact, relied on it entirely, have you not, as the main basis of your opinion in this case?'

'No.'

'What objective signs of insanity are there in the prisoner?'

'I should have to repeat all my evidence to show that.'

'Far be it from me to ask you to do that,' said the attorney general, probably speaking for everyone else in the court. 'What objective signs of insanity are there apart from what the prisoner has said to you?'

Now the doctor could pull academic rank on counsel. 'There are no such things as objective signs of insanity; it is one of the oldest fallacies,' he said with a thin-lipped smile.

'Then you are relying in the main upon what the prisoner said to you?'

'No, I am relying in the main on my lifelong knowledge of such cases and my observations of a cumulative series of symptoms, as I said.'

'Do you attach importance to the dreams?'

'Yes, I attach great importance.'

'Whether this man dreamed or not is a matter you can only judge by what he told you? You said a moment ago that he was incapable of speaking the truth?'

'Yes.'

'The other matter was the drinking of the urine? You know from the consultations you have had with Dr Matheson that although he has been watched he has only been seen to drink his urine on one occasion, when he publicly demonstrated to a doctor that he was able to do it? I must put it to you that there is no evidence at all that he persistently or consistently drinks his urine, apart from what the prisoner told you and Dr Matheson's account of a particular demonstration?'

'Yes,' agreed Dr Yellowlees.

The knife was starting to go further in. The attorney general now turned to John Haigh's previous convictions for conspiracy to defraud, forgery, uttering and obtaining money by forged documents and obtaining money by false pretences. He asked if it was impossible that the accused might have deceived Dr Yellowlees about his dreams and other symptoms when he had been so successful in deceiving others. The doctor replied that he didn't think he'd been deceived but might well have been.

The attorney general said that there had been some question of heredity in all this and asked if the doctor had seen the father's statement. He said he had. When pushed further as to whether the statement helped the doctor on the question of sanity, Dr Yellowlees had to admit he couldn't remember anything in the statement. Sir David then interrupted to say he'd never seen the father's statement and there followed a kerfuffle, with the judge weighing in to say that someone in the prosecution team could probably lend him a copy but it was unlikely it was going to become evidence.

A copy was then produced and Sir Hartley asked the witness to look at the following paragraph:

During the time that John was at home he was a good boy, and right up to the time he left home he never misbehaved. He had very good health, and there was nothing wrong with him mentally. He got on very well with other boys, but I think he was too generous.

Sir Hartley asked whether this didn't destroy the idea of a boy without friends living a solitary life with mental problems, to which the doctor replied that the last thing relatives of someone suspected to be insane will admit is the presence of a family history of insanity.

Mr Justice Humphreys butted in here to say it was his experience that when a person is charged with murder and is setting up a defence of insanity, his relatives usually are willing to help him by saying there has been a great deal of insanity in the family.

Then came the question as to whether the witness had asked John Haigh about how much profit he had made out of the murders of the McSwans and Hendersons. Dr Yellowlees replied that he hadn't asked, although he was aware of it in the various statements but did not think it was of any importance whether or not he'd made any money.

Next the attorney general referred again to the dreams and whether the accused had elaborated on these from time to time, and Dr Yellowlees agreed he had. Was the doctor aware, he asked, that Haigh had not actually mentioned the dreams while he was at Lewes prison? Didn't this suggest that he'd been working up the facts? In response, Dr Yellowlees agreed that he was working up the facts but only because he couldn't help it.

A picture was building of a psychiatrist who, however eminent and experienced, hadn't asked the common-sense questions that most of us would have asked. Why didn't Dr Yellowlees ask John Haigh why he didn't say anything about these bleeding Christ and bowls of blood dreams while he was at Lewes prison? Why didn't he question Haigh about the obvious motive of making a lot of money from these murders to live an extravagant lifestyle? Did the urge to drink blood just coincide each time with the money running out? What about the Hendersons – did he get the urge to drink blood twice that day or did he want to prevent Mrs Henderson going to the police about the disappearance of her husband?

32

Throughout Dr Yellowlees's evidence the assumption had been that paranoia was indeed 'a mental disease' as required under the M'Naghten Rules. As Dr Yellowlees was not willing to give a view as to whether or not the accused knew he was doing wrong (an essential element of the definition), then to show that paranoia was less than a disease would sound the death knell – literally in John Haigh's case – for the defence of insanity.

Sir Hartley paused before the kill. 'I have observed,' he started quietly, 'that throughout this case you have not referred to this man as suffering from a mental disease. Is paranoia a disease at all?'

'Yes, paranoia is a profound mental disease.'

'The view taken by the book to which you have referred as the classic is rather different, is it not?'

This was a reference to Professor Eugenio Tanzi's *A Textbook of Mental Diseases* that Dr Yellowlees had constantly referred to during his evidence as the big authority on paranoia. The professor was also someone under whom he had trained. Sir Hartley now picked up the tome. 'I am reading from page 746. "Paranoia is not a true disease but is an intellectual anomaly." Do you agree with that?' he asked.

'No, it is simply a matter of words. It really is very easy,' replied the doctor, and went on to explain that most mental diseases produce a physical alteration in the brain as an organ. The exception is paranoia, and someone might suffer from paranoia for fifty years with no visible changes to the brain whatsoever.

Sir Hartley tried another tack. 'Would you call him a lunatic in everyday language?'

'Among doctors I would.'

Sir Harley picked up the considerable weight of the textbook again. 'Professor Tanzi says the paranoiac is an anomalous being, but he is not a lunatic in the common meaning of the term. Paranoia is to be regarded as a simple development anomaly, the product of a passionate temperament and a methodical and pedantic mind. You do not agree with that?'

'I do not agree with any sentence taken out of context applying to anyone who died thirty years ago. But I agree entirely with the views expressed in that chapter, and indeed it was I who discovered how important it was and brought the book here. That is why I got a copy of the book,' said Dr Yellowlees, tiring of the hostility.

'You appreciate why I am asking you the question, do you not?' asked schoolmaster and now executioner Sir Hartley.

'Not quite.'

'You are very familiar, are you not, with the legal definition of insanity as far as the question of criminal responsibility is concerned? The first thing that has to be established is that the accused is suffering from a disease of the mind. You appreciated that this is what my question was directed to, did you not?'

'Yes, for a moment I did not, but I see now.'

Sir Harley went on with the rest of the definition and the question as to whether the accused knew he was doing wrong. 'Is your difficulty really this, that you realise that from the preparations which the prisoner made in this case he must have known it was wrong?'

'No,' replied Dr Yellowlees emphatically, 'if that had been my difficulty I should not have dreamed of coming to give evidence.'

'Is it your opinion that he was acting in obedience to a higher law?'

'Yes, he said so.'

'But he realised the law of this country was binding on him?'

'I am not satisfied about that; I wish I could be. I am not satisfied that he did not know it was wrong.'

'Whether he believed he was acting under the guidance of a higher power or not, did he believe that according to the law of this country what he was doing was wrong?'

'He cannot have, if he believed he was acting under a power above the law.'

'I am asking you to look at the facts and tell the jury whether there is any doubt that he must have known that according to English law he was preparing to do and subsequently had done something which was wrong?'

'I will say yes to that if you say punishable by law instead of wrong.'

'Punishable by law and, therefore, wrong by the law of this country?'

'Yes, I think he knew that.'

Sir Hartley sat down with the air of a tennis player winning game, set and match without having to break a sweat. He leaned forward to thrust the Tanzi tome back into the bookshelf of case reports and authorities shared by counsel.

Sir David Maxwell Fyfe got to his feet and tried to collect some of the broken pieces of his witness's evidence. He asked prosecution counsel if he might borrow back the Tanzi and opened it at one of the marked pages.

'Have you ever given evidence before on a case of pure paranoia?' he asked Dr Yellowlees.

'Never.'

'Is it because of the difficulty arising out of pure paranoia that you are not prepared to answer the question as to whether the accused knew that he was doing what was wrong?' asked Sir David.

'That is so,' came the reply.

Sir David turned to page 720 of Tanzi to quote how 'the paranoiac with delusions of ambition is comforted by the presence of fetishes and guardian angels' and, three pages later, how 'paranoiac delusion is the fantastic product of an egocentric but lucid spirit which abandons itself without restraint to the mysticism of primitive man'.

'Yes, I agree with that entirely,' said Dr Yellowlees, without expanding.

Other than having Dr Yellowlees confirm that he received full co-operation from the prison doctor Dr Matheson, Sir David said that was all the evidence he was going to call.

Whether anyone in court understood a word of what had just been quoted, let alone agreed with it, apart from Dr Yellowlees, was answered in the rather chilling reply by the attorney general when asked by the judge whether he wanted to call any evidence in rebuttal to what had been said.

'On that evidence, my lord, when the time comes I shall submit there is nothing to rebut.'

33

All that was left in the trial of The King *v.* John George Haigh was for both sides to give their closing speeches and then the judge his summing up before the jury was asked to go and consider their verdict.

For the defence the task of making a closing speech to a jury already saturated with prosecution evidence, which in the main went unchallenged, and hours of expert evidence for the defence, which for the most part they didn't understand, was not an easy one.

John Haigh himself had not been called to give evidence and had been left in the dock to complete his crossword; nor had a member of the family or a friend been called to talk about John's childhood to account for what happened later. His parents were too elderly and by the sounds of it would simply have said that John was the perfect son, a good Christian singing in the cathedral choir, happy and generous to a fault. As to his friends, well, it sounded as if he'd disposed of most of them, and if they had survived they would probably have said very much the same thing as his parents.

For the jury, after facing the factual horrors of the killings and the banal and cheerful way John Haigh had gone about it all with his meticulous preparation and disposal of the bodies, the waiting was nearly over. Some members of the jury had lost track of exactly the number of people he was meant to have killed, and the best explanation of how he got caught on this the sixth victim, Mrs Durand-Deacon, seemed nothing more than carelessness, otherwise he might have gone on and on, funding a nice little lifestyle thank you very much. Now he was saying he was mad, and a posh and almost incoherent doctor had been brought down from London to say so.

The jury had listened to equally posh barristers, whom one or two jury members recognised from photos in the newspapers of the Nuremberg trials at the end of the war. Well, they sorted out Goering and company, even though some of them had said they were mad and obeying orders from a higher force. They'd all been strung up, and even that was too good for them. Now Haigh seemed to be trying the same thing.

Sir David could guess the scepticism in the minds of the jury and decided to ask them not to be too quick in either saying anyone who killed deserved what he got or anyone who acted like this was probably mad, however helpful this second course might be to his client. Instead he suggested they try to steer a course somewhere between these two views and that if anyone was going to be able to name a paranoiac then it would be Dr Henry Yellowlees. He might have got a mauling from the prosecution, but he was a man who could spot a paranoiac when he saw one.

'Dr Yellowlees, after all, is a gentleman who has devoted his whole life to this study,' said Sir David. 'I know that in modern days less importance is attached to university qualifications and fellowships than may have been the usual line of thought some time ago. But more important than that is the practical experience, a man who has been consulted on all the problems of mental difficulty that come up in the army of the field, a man who has been in at least four institutions, whose name is a byword in the treatment of insanity.'

Sir David then went through the foundation of paranoia and the existence of a paranoid constitution. He went through his client's childhood background, the exclusion of friends and the narrowness in his upbringing. He described him losing touch with real life and then the change in religious atmosphere from Plymouth Brethren to High Church at the cathedral and how this would have affected a growing boy. He spoke of the dreams of the bleeding Christ and bowls of blood.

He mentioned again the drinking of urine and how this for a paranoiac reverts to the practices of savage tribes. 'The important point is that the people who do it, like the prisoner here, have not studied Sir James Frazer's *Golden Bough* or some other repository of savage practices. I have not read it myself, I doubt whether any of you have read it and I doubt whether any of you, unless you have served in West Africa or some similar place, would be able to invent practices of savage tribes.'

Similarly Sir David asked how anyone could make up a dream like the dreams they'd heard about in court that day. He made the point that the prosecution had neither called any expert evidence to say the accused had not had these dreams nor indeed challenged anything else said by Dr Yellowlees.

He mentioned the absence of any sexual gratification or motive and tried to take head-on the question of financial gain and say the accused was living his own life in parallel and had to slip back into that from time to time.

Finally he quoted from Erskine, which Sir David had swotted up the previous evening after the reference to him on the previous day by the prosecution, that 'delusion where there is no frenzy or raving madness, is the true character of insanity'. Haigh was under the delusion that he was specifically controlled by the divine mystic force behind the world operating on his mind, and from that came the delusion that this force compelled and demanded that he should commit the murders and drink this blood.

Sir David sat down, gathering his gown around him, after saying that if he'd taken three times as long to say what he had – probably the most terrible thing with which he could threaten the court – 'it would still be the duty and the glory of English justice that anyone who has a mind so clearly displaying these abnormalities and disorders should have that mind considered freely and dispassionately by a jury of his peers. I believe my client has had that experience, and if he has had that experience I leave the verdict in your hands.'

Leaving the jury still uncertain what Sir David was talking about.

34

S ir Hartley Shawcross had hinted, at the end of his cross-examination of Dr Yellowlees, how he would frame his summing-up to the jury. He was faced, after all, with an accused who admitted to murder but claimed he was insane and in doing so declined to give evidence and called no witnesses except a psychiatrist. This psychiatrist had proved wobbly on the question of the patient suffering from a disease of the mind but if he did suffer from a disease of the mind then was unwilling to say whether he knew he was doing wrong, the other vital part of the definition of insanity as a defence.

In not calling any psychiatrist of their own to rebut what Dr Yellowlees was saying the prosecution were taking a risk, but if there was nothing to rebut then not calling their own expert was quite logical. The attorney general had watched Dr Yellowlees and the defence counsel tangle themselves up in a web of higher forces and guardian angels, and a few words now of common sense, with as few technicalities as possible, would probably do the trick.

'Members of the jury, the only issue remaining in this case, if indeed any substantial issue remains in it all,' started the attorney general, 'is the issue of the prisoner's sanity. You may think that the speculations of Dr Yellowlees are based on assumptions which are not proved in evidence and which you may think to be non-existent in fact.'

Every member of the jury could understand what he was saying, and probably every member of the jury agreed with him.

'The theories, unsubstantiated in any way, about this prisoner's childhood, about his early environment, the account of his dreams, the urge to drink blood and these other matters, are matters dependent, and dependent solely, upon the statements which the prisoner has given to his medical advisers, the prisoner a man, as Dr Yellowlees himself has said in the witness-box, whose word is not to be believed.

'Once you knock away one or two of these assumptions,' added Sir Hartley, 'which are unsupported by any kind of evidence before you, then the whole edifice of medical speculation and theory falls to the ground.'

The jury straightened in their seats. Thank God, someone at last was talking sense. The attorney general, someone who sounded so important, talked their language. He was of them, and they could stop feeling guilty about not understanding much of what Dr Yellowlees was saying and his cast of bleeding Christs, bowls of blood, mysticism and fallen angels. For God's sake, this man had murdered six people, or was it nine? Whatever it was he couldn't just say he was mad and look forward to a cushy life in Broadmoor. Indeed, this was one of the questions he put to the police when he was first interviewed.

The attorney general seized the moment. 'It is very easy for doctors, and indeed even for counsel, to say that a man who committed such a crime as this must be mad. If all responsibility for wicked and criminal conduct is not to be cast aside, the law, which in certain circumstances admits insanity as an excuse, must be certain and must be defined and must be strictly administered because, if it were otherwise, at once all sorts of vague and unsubstantial theories might be let so as to provide excuses for what has been done, and the whole law of criminal responsibility would become so unreliable, so vague and so uncertain that no tests at all could be laid down for juries to apply and administer in the circumstances of particular cases.'

In short, he seemed to be saying, believe this and you'd believe anything. He added that if you allowed these sorts of things to go through then the administration of the criminal law would pass out of the hands of the courts and juries to medical specialists in a science where a little knowledge is a dangerous thing.

He said that he had not called any evidence to challenge Dr Yellowlees because his evidence was conclusive in itself that this prisoner was not insane; he knew full well that he was killing Mrs Durand-Deacon; that killing her was wrong; and that he could be punished if he was caught. Once Dr Yellowlees admitted that this man knew he was doing wrong, that was an end to the case. This was a simple case where a man had discovered the perfect way of concealing murder and tried to do it again. It was a case where sanity is only raised as an issue because the charge was murder and no other defence was open.

Before he finally sat down, Sir Hartley, like any prosecuting counsel in a capital offence case before 1965, was aware that in asking a jury to convict a person of murder he was asking them to send the accused to the gallows, albeit now an expert operation carried out in private in a prison but an execution nevertheless, whatever euphemism you wanted to use. The jury, like everyone else in court, had been watching John Haigh in the dock, sometimes reading his newspaper or doing the crossword, sometimes smiling to himself or at the jury, sometimes jotting notes that he passed forward to his solicitor. When DS Heslin said in evidence that he had to force the door of the workroom in order to get in to search there for the first time, John scribbled a note saying 'why not get this man for breaking and entering?' Then there was another note saying 'carthorse' was the solution to the anagram of 'orchestra' in his crossword. Whatever the little man's failings, he always seemed courteous and happy, with a certain sense of humour. He probably was mad in his way – as anyone who disposes of at least six people, all of them his friends, would have to be. Despite the horrors, they couldn't help liking him.

Aware of all this, Sir Hartley finished his speech. 'Members of the jury, your duty, your *duty* to which you are sworn,' he emphasised the word, 'the duty which you have been discharging these last two days, is to administer the law according to the evidence. It is often, I dare say, an unpleasant duty in many ways, but it would be more unpleasant if you were to depart from that duty and from what you are sworn to do. I shall ask you to say that in this case your duty and your oath, your duty to yourselves, your duty to the State, leaves you no possible alternative but to find this man guilty of the offence with which he is charged.'

Having used the word no fewer than eight times, the attorney general completed his duty in prosecuting John George Haigh and sat down.

35

In summing up at the end of a trial the judge has three main tasks to perform: to disentangle the evidence put forward by each side and present the arguments in a balanced and lucid way; to apply the law to those arguments; and to try to give the jury some sort of structure on which to base their discussion in the jury room. In doing all this he or she must use ordinary language rather than legal or technical jargon. It is a tricky operation, and if he gets it wrong then he may provide the basis for an appeal.

It is also the first time the jury have heard the judge string more than a couple of sentences together during the course of the trial, apart from a few questions to counsel and the warning to the jury at the end of the first day not to discuss the case at home. Mr Justice Humphreys, a man in his early eighties whose career at the bar had covered six decades and five monarchs, had already shown himself quick to take up points during the trial, so the jury knew he wasn't there in a passive role, but they'd need some help in trying to discover how mad a person had to be before they were considered insane by law.

'That is the importance of having twelve persons, probably unknown to each other, brought by chance, by the lot of the ballot, into a jury box to answer this question: here is a lot of evidence on this or that or the other according to different people; will you tell us what is the truth? We want your opinion as to what are the true facts,' said the judge in his opening remarks.

The first question facing the jury, he said, was to ask if Haigh murdered Mrs Durand-Deacon. Usually in this sort of case he would say nothing, but here according even to the defence's one and only witness, the man had been shown to be utterly unreliable. Nevertheless Humphreys reminded the jury of a few facts that the prosecution said conclusively show that he killed her, including him being seen that day in Crawley with Mrs Durand-Deacon and then later without her, the quantities of sulphuric acid, Haigh selling her jewellery and her remains being found in the yard outside the storeroom at Leopold Road.

As to the question of insanity, no jury is ever called on to say if someone is insane, that is a question to be left to the doctors. Instead what they were being asked to decide is whether under the M'Naghten Rules the accused is to be punished for a criminal act because it was a conscious act, not merely because he'd done some act which had injured someone else when, for example, having an epileptic fit or sleepwalking. He explained how in 1843 poor Daniel M'Naghten was living in Scotland, a decent and respectable man but suffering from delusions of persecution where he believed people were conspiring against him and making his life hell. One of these people he thought was Sir Robert Peel, the then prime minister, and so he came down to Downing Street and shot the first person to emerge from the prime minister's residence, and this person happened to be his secretary rather than the prime minster himself.

While M'Naghten was obviously mad by any standard, the question was if he was sufficiently mad not to be responsible for his crime. Chief Justice Tindal, the judge at the time, said, 'The question is whether this man had the competent use of his understanding so that he knew that he was doing a wicked and wrong thing. If he was not sensible that it was a violation of the law of God or man, undoubtedly he was not responsible for the act or liable to any punishment whatever.'

Doesn't that read to you, asked Humphreys now, almost exactly as the law today? It is the same thing, had he the competent use of his understanding so as to enable him to appreciate what he was doing was wrong? Did Haigh know at the time he shot this lady whom he had inveigled from London down to Crawley that it was a wrong thing to do?

Even though Dr Yellowlees had said in the end that Haigh knew what he was doing and that it was wrong, the judge told the jury it was up to them to make up their own minds. The judge had known a jury halfway through a trial to say they didn't want to hear anything more because, looking at the accused's behaviour in the dock, he was clearly mad as a hatter.

After going through Dr Yellowlees's evidence, the judge recalled that Dr Yellowlees firmly believed that Haigh was suffering from a disease of the mind, namely paranoia, while the prosecution pointed to Professor Tanzi in his book saying paranoia was not a disease of the mind. The judge said he didn't want this case to be decided on this point and suggested that it would be better to call it a disease of the mind for the purposes of this case: it wouldn't be satisfactory to convict someone of murder, if he was otherwise very insane, if that particular form of insanity was not recognised by the medical profession as a disease.

The judge made the point that the questions of Haigh drinking his own urine, dreams of forests of crucifixes and the drinking the blood of his victims were based on what he had told Dr Yellowlees without any back-up evidence, while mention of his previous convictions would not normally be introduced and were only introduced here because the defence wished this.

The judge referred to Haigh telling the doctor he had a destiny to fulfil, namely killing people, and that he was an instrument of an outside power. When the doctor was asked whether this man knew what he was doing was wrong, the doctor said that no psychiatrist could answer that question unless he'd lived with the man many years. If you understand that answer, said the judge, then you understand something I do not. The doctor was asked if he'd ever said in a previous case that he couldn't say whether a person he'd examined couldn't tell whether an act was wrong or not to which he replied 'no, he'd never said so in a previous case'. However, he did say in the end that Haigh believed what he was doing was wrong and punishable by English law.

The judge told the jury that because a man commits two or three murders does not mean he is insane. He reminded them of 'The Brides in the Bath' case not so long ago, where the accused was convicted of three separate murders of three wives and nobody suggested he was insane. As to Haigh's later reference to killing another three people, this rested entirely on his statement and the police said they knew nothing about it.

Before the members of the jury retired, the judge offered them anything they wanted to take in the way of exhibits or any of the statements or photographs. There were a total of fifty-six exhibits, most of them still sitting on or under a table at the front of the court, below the judge's bench. They made a sad and desultory collection of clothing, photographs, jewellery, handbags, cosmetics, a gasmask case, service revolver, stirrup pump, and rubber apron and gloves, set out on their stall with all the subtlety of a jumble sale. Besides items of her clothing and jewellery, Mrs Durand-Deacon in person was represented by two and a half gallstones, some flecks of blood on a strip of whitewash and a set of dentures.

The reply from the jury to the judge's offer to take exhibits with them suggested they hadn't been listening to the offer to take the exhibits. 'My lord, it is the jury's desire – would you allow us to retire?' replied the foreman.

The judge looked back from under his wig at him and stuck out his lower lip. Were he a schoolmaster he might have told him to wake up and listen. Instead he replied, 'Certainly. I was only asking whether you wanted to take with you anything that has been produced in the course of the case. If you do want anything while you are in your room, just knock at the door and the bailiff will let me know and you will have them.'

With that the twelve members of the jury, under the auspices of the bailiffs, filed out of court and over the corridor to the jury room. They were tired and thirsty at the end of a second long day in a warm court listening to difficult and occasionally incomprehensible medical evidence, long speeches from the barristers and finally the summing-up from the judge himself. This followed the previous day with its evidence from thirty-three witnesses and horrors that, although anticipated by the newspapers and particularly the *Daily Mirror*, were suddenly made real by coming face to face with a serial murderer and the remains of a lady who might have been one's aunt or granny, going about her daily life until she entered the clutches of the man who might have been one's bank manager or stockbroker.

36

Mr Justice Humphreys returned to his chambers in the court building at 4.25 p.m. and gratefully accepted the offer of a cup of tea from his clerk. He was weary but pleased with the work of the court over the last two days. Both senior counsel were old campaigners and the attorney general in particular had done a good job keeping it all together and not allowing himself to get bogged down with the medical evidence. He wondered how much of the medical evidence the jury had understood – probably not much and they'd have the time now to go through it before they considered a verdict. The truth was no one really knew how a jury went about its task of arriving at a verdict, and doubtless they would be as tired as he was. He planned to give them at least half an hour, until five o'clock, and then send them off home to start afresh in the morning.

The judge took off his wig and threw it on to his desk. He'd been pleased to sit in this case and had his eye on it from the start. Now in his eighty-second year, he thought he should probably chuck it all in for good, but as long as the occasional case like this came up it seemed worth soldiering on. There were still interesting decisions to make, like turfing this case out of London, back to Lewes where it belonged. There was also the decision today, to tell the jury not to get too worked up about whether paranoia was or was not a disease of the mind. He wasn't going to hang a man just because academics argued about the status of an illness. Did Haigh know what he was doing was wrong? That was the thing: was he mad as a hatter? Was he homosexual like one of his first clients, Oscar Wilde? Like Haigh, Wilde was married and similarly cavalier about his trial.

The trouble was that he, as Mr Justice Humphreys, might run out of interesting cases and want to live a quieter life as Mr Travers Humphreys. He'd already written one book about his cases and there'd be another in his retirement. The question was where to spend his retirement? If he ever became a widower then what about the Onslow Court Hotel?

He felt, in a funny sort of way, there was some mutual admiration between him and John George Haigh. He'd noticed Haigh hang on every word of his closing speech, nodding occasionally, eyes bright blue and taking in every word, and for his part the judge slightly envied Haigh's way of life in the Onslow Court Hotel. The hotel was obviously luxurious, well run and supportive to a mainly elderly clientele. The residents were, to use the cliché, growing old gracefully. The victim herself seemed a woman of culture and learning, with interests ranging from Francis Bacon to the possible manufacture of fingernails. Someone had told him that she was once active in the suffragette movement and had even hurled a brick through someone's window and spent the night in the cells. Haigh himself seemed to live a good life, joining in with all this. With a dark humour that often came up in horror trials, he realised if Haigh went down on this one there would be a couple of vacancies at the Onslow Court Hotel.

His only regret was that he hadn't had the chance to put a question to Haigh or see him give evidence. It was usually not appropriate to let someone with mental problems give evidence and anyway, as he pointed out in his summing-up, the jury was not there to decide if someone was insane, that was up to the doctors. Still, Haigh's voice sounded surprisingly high when he pleaded not guilty, belying his stockbroker image. Had he really been doing the crossword up there in the dock during the trial or was this a front to impress the court? What was in these notes he handed down to his solicitor, notes that Haigh found amusing but his solicitor didn't?

There were a lot of things they didn't know about Mr Haigh, and may now never know if the verdict went against him. In a funny sort of way he, as a judge, would not particularly regret Haigh being found insane and bundled off to Broadmoor rather than being executed. People seemed to like him – you could see by the way Haigh and his police guards chatted and even shared a joke, the genial smile nearly always on his lips, the respect between him and his solicitor and counsel. The man obviously had talent, he was an inventor and musician, and talented forger, and on several occasions he had committed the perfect murder, undetected until he became careless, or even indifferent. He was the sort of case Broadmoor might like to take on. He could see Haigh fitting into Broadmoor, in the same way he fitted into the Onslow Court Hotel.

Still, they would know Haigh's fate tomorrow once the jury had had a good night's sleep and then settled themselves back into the jury room in the morning to sift through the evidence.

So it was with some surprise that after taking only a couple of sips at his tea, his clerk returned to say the jury was coming back into court. The judge assumed this was to ask for a direction or for some of the exhibits; for example, he wondered how a man the size of Haigh got a 14-stone body into a 40gal drum. But his surprise turned to shock when his clerk said he understood the jury had come to a verdict.

It was 4.40 p.m., only fifteen minutes after they had left court to start their deliberations.

John Haigh looked across the courtroom to the jury, a smile still on his face, but not one member of the jury looked back. The clerk to the court asked the prisoner and foreman to stand. 'Members of the jury,' he asked, 'are you agreed upon your verdict?'

'We are,' replied the foreman.

'Do you find the prisoner, John George Haigh, guilty or not guilty of murdering Mrs Durand-Deacon, or do you find him guilty but insane?'

'Guilty of murdering Mrs Durand-Deacon.'

'Is that the verdict of you all?'

'That is the unanimous verdict.'

The clerk now turned to John Haigh. 'Prisoner at the Bar, have you anything to say why sentence of death should not be passed on you according to law?'

'Nothing at all,' he replied.

The judge's clerk produced the black cloth, which he proceeded to place across the top of the judge's wig like a waiter laying a tablecloth.

The judge's chaplain, a local bishop, fortunately had delayed going home until the jury themselves had been dismissed for the night and now sat on one side of the judge. The sheriff also took his place beside the judge.

Mr Justice Humphreys had delivered the death sentence before on many occasions but was not word perfect. He read from a typed card tucked inside his notebook. 'John George Haigh, the sentence of the Court upon you is that you be taken from this place to a lawful prison, and thence to a place of execution, and there you suffer death by hanging, and that your body be buried within the precincts of the prison in which you shall have been last confined before your execution; and may the Lord have mercy upon your soul.'

'Amen,' intoned the chaplain, and the prisoner, still smiling, was taken down to the cells.

37

The execution suite, as it was known, at Wandsworth prison, to where John Haigh was transferred on the evening after his trial, consisted of a room rather larger than a cell with two windows looking over pine trees on the outside of the prison wall, three chairs, two doors, a table and a bed. The chairs were for the prisoner and the two warders who were on twenty-four-hour 'death watch', taken from a team of six prison officers on eight-hour shifts. One door led out into the corridor at the end of which was a lavatory and bathroom, while the other led straight to the gallows directly on the other side of the wall.

On the table was a pack of cards and a chess set for the prisoner to while away the time, together with some books approved by the governor. Books could be sent in to the prisoner by family or friends, but once again would need approval by the governor, who would also approve letters coming in or out of the condemned suite. There was also a standard daily issue of a pint of beer and ten cigarettes, although the prisoner could smoke his own if he wished.

Now he was no longer a remand prisoner, John had to give up his civilian suit and shirt and wear regulation prison clothing, which was difficult for a man whose sartorial sense was important to him and a reason to put him off having visitors. In fact, he made this clear to his parents in his letters, implying that one reason for them not to visit him now in prison was his rather grim prison clothes with all buttons and fasteners removed.

Otherwise he took to life in the execution suite like a duck to water, busying himself with writing letters to Barbara, his parents and his solicitor. There was the continuing life story to write for the *News of the World* and daily meetings and discussions with the prison chaplain, the Reverend Baden Ball, whom he knew from his Dartmoor days. On Sundays John would attend the service in the prison chapel but this time as a condemned prisoner, without making any contact with his fellow prisoners. This was achieved by him sitting with his two warders in a side room in the chapel, looking through a grilled window into the nave. Sunday 24 July was his fortieth birthday and he received a selection of cards and presents; that it was his birthday made the chapel service even more poignant, bringing back memories of prayers in the house with his parents and in the choir at Wakefield Cathedral.

His only complaint about the executive suite, reducing it perhaps from a five- to a four-star rating, were the warders, whom he considered dull, incapable of interesting talk and well below his intellectual level. These death-watch warders were taken from volunteers in the service, usually outside London, fulfilling their main function of preventing the condemned harming themselves and keeping a log of their activities.

On his first full day in the prison John received a visit from the prison governor, Major Benke, who ran the prison with military, and largely successful, precision. However, the visit was rather marred by an incident where John went into the lavatory of the condemned suite to give a required urine sample but instead filled his drinking glass with his urine and had to be stopped from drinking it by the governor.

But first there was work to do and letters to write. A week after his trial John's mind was very far from the hereafter. On 26 July he was writing to his solicitor in Horsham about the patents on his inventions, and only then did he allow himself to reflect on the trial itself:

> Messrs Eager & Sons
> 8 North Street
> Horsham, Sy.
>
> Dear Mr Eager
>   Would you care to look into the Reidie and Gross file.
> I received a letter just before leaving Brixton from
> them advising me that they had prepared the application
> for the restitution of the Hindustan Haumer Patent. They
> were apparently sending this first to Child & Child to
> receive Mrs Fenerhurd's signature and then on to me.
> I have not received this yet and therefore I think you

might investigate this question as there is I presume a
time limit set for that.

I was interested in Morris's views on procedure and
shall hope that you will expand these further when you
come along.

You were interested in my reaction to proceedings
last week. In the first instance I think that it was a
good thing that I had that Xword to do or I should have
been very bored with the first day's proceedings, having
heard that evidence so often before. I became much more
interested when Yellowlees and Sir David opened up the
spiritual theme of the case. I do think that Yellowlees
had a good point in mind when he made it clear that I
could have hardly thought at the age of 15 or so that
I should eventually have arrived at the condemned cell
at Wandsworth, and therefore I could not at that age
begin to spin a web of circumstances to fit the case 25
years after. But I do wish he had developed the theme
more fully. Madness is however a label which has been
applied to all men of distinction and to all those who
have found their metier outside the realm of common
thought. So that although I cannot agree with him there
I can forgive him. After all did they not accuse Christ
of being mad too? And only because he like myself had
a clearer perception of the infinite mind than the rest
of unenlightened and infertile humanity. And so finally
he was put to death. So have thousands since for their
spiritual convictions. Therefore I find myself with no
bitterness against those who have brought a verdict of
guilty according to their law. For as Christ said before
Pilate they had no power to do so – and to think out
their verdict – if it were not given from above. So,
though there was much I might have said when asked to do
so I did as a sheep before her shearer is dumb open not
my mouth [sic]. It was an effort to refrain from audible
laughter when the Judge donned his black cap. He looked
for all the world like a sheep with its head peering out

from under a rhubarb leaf. It was on my tongue to say
'Don your fool's cap and get on with the farce'. I may
die – as men know it – but as a participle of the infinite
my spirit will live and I shall return in another body
to build a greater church. For have I not gone this way
before? Was I not burned at the stake as a Wharlock
[sic] in Salem? I laugh at death and return to earth to
continue my spiritual sacrifices.

Yours Truly,

J.G. Haigh

Three days later John was writing to his parents on matters spiritual to
explain his own actions:

To use your own phraseology God moves in a mysterious way.
So that being led by an undesirable urge I was not given
to consider what discomfort this might cause either to
myself or to others. Spiritual conviction does not take
into account the opinion or feelings of opposed thought.
When the great spirit of infinity constrained Israel to
go out and slay each man his brother he did not take into
account the injunction of Moses: Thou shall not kill. It
may have been contrary to the moral laws of this land but
then moral laws are purely relative. It is not so in every
country of the world. The spiritual conviction of the
individual is above mere (unenlightened) man made laws.
When one is convinced of propulsion by higher power one
disregards man. One does not even think about it.

The religious excuse to his parents strengthened as the date of execution
drew nearer, so with five days to go he wrote:

This case … may make them realise that religious freedom is
not yet complete. If so I shall go down in history as another
martyr to my faith as great as Cranmer, or any other.

Meanwhile there were letters to his counsel and doctor:

1st August 1949

Dear Sir David,

I would like you to know that I appreciate the efforts you have made on my behalf. Although I myself could not always understand why you adopted one line and not another, I was nevertheless content to leave matters to your mature judgment and I was very satisfied that you finally put up a very good effort.

The fact that you visited me on more than one occasion confirmed that you were taking a very great personal interest in my case, a fact which evoked my even greater admiration of your reported ability.

I wish you, please, to accept my very warm thanks.

Yours truly,

J.G. Haigh

Finally to Dr Yellowlees, the only witness for the defence, on the same day:

Dear Sir,

I would like you to know that I appreciate the personal interest that you have taken and the effort you have made on my behalf, even though I cannot agree with your opinion. After all, all the outstanding personalities throughout human history have been considered odd: Confucius, Jesus Christ, Julius Caesar, Mahomet, Napoleon and even Hitler all possessed a greater perception of the infinite and a more lucid understanding of the omniscient mind. I am happy to inform you that my Mother in writing to me during the last week was able to confirm that my Headmistress at the High School and my Headmaster at the Trueman both reported that I was not all the normal boy. How could it be otherwise in the product of an angel and one of the few men who ever sinned?

I do therefore have the utmost admiration for your greater perception and am grateful to you for your courageous exposition of it.

Yours truly,

J.G. Haigh

38

Meanwhile Stafford Somerfield, the *News of the World* reporter who had landed the coup of having John Haigh write his story exclusively for his newspaper, had not only attended the trial in Lewes but corresponded with John's parents. After a week of John entering Wandsworth, he heard from them saying they had received a letter from George, as they called their son, enclosing a visitor's permit, but due to their age, health and distress coming down to see him was impossible, and anyway they thought this would only grieve him. Would Somerfield go for them and tell him 'he is our dearest treasure on earth … and we commit him to the God of All Graces'.

So, after a little trouble as it was prison policy not to allow members of the press in to visit prisoners, Somerfield obtained a visiting order on 4 August, granted because the parents had asked him to visit on their behalf.

On the afternoon of Friday 5 August, Somerfield presented himself at the prison with his visiting order in hand, not quite knowing what one said to a condemned prisoner. He repeated to the warders that he understood the prison regulations and that he was there to give a message to the prisoner from his mother. He was then led out of the main waiting room, into the prison yard, round the side of the building and up an iron staircase like a fire escape. A door was opened with a lot a jangling of keys and they entered a bleak room, where Somerfield was sat down at a table facing a window surrounded by a grille. John was sitting on the other side of this window with his two warders.

John was looking well, almost tanned. In a grey jacket and white open-necked shirt, he still managed to look smart. 'Good afternoon,' said John. 'I've been wanting to see you for a long time.'

Somerfield's nervousness about the meeting vanished at once. They might have being having tea in the Tudor Room at the Onslow Court Hotel. John put him at his ease, and they used the meeting to discuss John's personal affairs, his finances and where he wanted his remaining property to go and to whom.

Throughout the meeting, scheduled to last no longer than half an hour, Somerfield couldn't help noticing John's pianist's manicured hands and his slightly high-pitched but not unpleasant voice. At the end of the interview John said he'd like to see him again, on his own account and not as a messenger from his parents, and this wish was officially granted by the governor at 3 p.m. on 9 August, just eighteen hours before John was scheduled to be executed.

This second visit was more relaxing for Stafford Somerfield. Instead of a grilling from the prison staff as to why he wanted to see John, they knew him from the previous visit and put up no resistance. 'You know the way, I think. You've been here before,' said the senior officer as they climbed the same staircase and passed through the same door into the same bleak room.

This time John looked different, as if he'd been woken up during an afternoon nap. He was wearing the same grey suit and white shirt, but the trousers had lost their crease and his eyes were puffy, with dark rings under them. Nevertheless, John was as welcoming as usual. '*So* nice of you to come,' he greeted them. 'I knew you would, of course, but I must admit you left it until the last moment.'

Somerfield had found him a book to read for his last night, Neville Cardus's autobiography, an account of the cricket and music critic's life which had been out a couple of years. John had read Cardus's books on music and attended some of the concerts reviewed by Cardus in his newspaper articles. They discussed the book for a while. 'But don't tell me any more. You'll spoil my reading tonight,' said John.

Still the same smile, with a deprecating shrug of the shoulders. Then John snapped into action. 'Now, time is getting short and I'd like you to take some notes of some things I would like you to do for me. I really would be most grateful.'

Somerfield wasn't quite sure if he was allowed to take notes, but he agreed with the warders that he'd pass them for approval by the governor. John dictated to Somerfield as if he was his secretary. 'All my possessions have now been numbered, and I'd like you to go through them,' he said, and went through, number by number, tagging items for his parents and his friends.

'This might strike you as slightly morbid,' he added. 'But I think it's necessary. I expect Madame Tussaud's will get in touch with you. And I should like this done properly. I suggest that I wear the green suit, red tie with green squares and green socks when they put my figure in the Chamber of Horrors.'

Somerfield finished making his note and put the piece of paper aside for a moment. John started to talk about the trial. 'Humphreys's summing-up was a masterpiece, wasn't it?' he said. 'I really enjoyed listening to it. But what a bore the rest of it was. Even the black cap business was ludicrous.'

He laughed and turned his attention to his parents. 'Please give them my love. I shall be writing to them tonight, but I should like you to go and give them a first-hand report of how I look and how I am behaving.'

For the first time Somerfield felt this was turning more into a hospital visit. 'You look extremely well; much better than I expected,' he said.

'Putting on weight a little, I'm afraid,' replied John, 'and that's because I'm sitting around so much and getting only an hour's exercise a day. But that's the least of my worries.'

A warder indicated there was only five minutes to go. John, with the last visitor he was to receive from outside the prison, turned the last five minutes into a seminar on belief. 'Let us discuss my theory and belief. I am fully convinced that at the centre of all being there is a Principle. Have you read my notes on this subject?'

Somerfield said that he had. 'Then tell me, do you agree with me?' asked John.

Somerfield floundered with an answer for a moment.

'I can see you are not convinced,' said John. 'A pity. The Principle is in connivance with the Being, so that the individual has no choice. What is accomplished thought carried out by the individual is purely by the wish of the Principle.'

Somerfield suggested that he preferred to believe that the individual still was able to influence his own destiny and that responsibility for one's actions lay largely within one's own power.

John finished the discussion by quoting word perfect, and without hesitation, from Ecclesiastes 3:15: 'That which hath been is now, and that which is to be hath already been; and God requireth that which is past.'

Finally Somerfield promised that he would get the items up to his parents, as this obviously concerned John.

'Fine,' he said. 'You're really very kind. Now what can I do for you?'

'Write to me tonight.'

'I will.'

'Time's up,' said the chief warder.

John immediately got up, flashed a smile at Somerfield, nodded his head and said simply goodbye.

Later in the evening John kept his word and wrote to Somerfield:

> Wandsworth Prison
> 9.8.1949
>
> Dear Mr Somerfield,
>
> I go forward to finish my mission in other forms. Has it occurred to you that liberty of religious thought is still not wholly existent in this country, that they still execute their heretics?
>
> Wishing you well,
>
> Yours Very Sincerely,
>
> John Haigh.

39

Permission for this last visit by Somerfield had been first requested by John the previous day when the governor of Wandsworth prison, Major Benke, arrived unannounced at the execution suite on the morning of Monday 8 August. The two warders stood when the governor walked in alone.

'Major, how nice to see you,' greeted John, sticking out a hand.

Major Benke solemnly shook hands and was offered a seat by one of the warders. 'Can we offer you anything?' asked John.

'No, thank you, Haigh. Unfortunately I am not able to offer you anything either. I have heard from the Home Secretary this morning saying that after consulting with the Home Office doctors he is not able to grant you a reprieve. I'm sorry.'

'Not at all, Major. So no route into Broadmoor, then?'

'I'm afraid not. The execution will therefore proceed on Wednesday as planned.'

'I see. Well, it's very kind of you to came along and tell me.'

Major Benke asked him if there was anything John wanted, and he asked then if Somerfield could come and see him on a no-holds-barred basis, without reporting restrictions. 'There is one other thing while we're on the subject — I'm concerned that things go well on Wednesday and I'm concerned that I might be heavier than I look.'

'I'm sorry, I'm not sure I understand.'

'The thing is, I've a springy step and look a lot lighter on my feet than I am. This is something your man in charge of the operation needs to take into account. I wondered if we could have some sort of rehearsal before Wednesday,' said John.

'I wouldn't mention these sort of details usually,' said a surprised governor. 'But rest assured the man in charge of the operation, as you put it, will make careful calculations beforehand to make sure it all goes smoothly and I have to say he's very experienced and always gets it right.'

'I wouldn't want anything to go wrong.'

Major Benke looked faintly bemused. 'I don't think we've ever had a request for a rehearsal before. But I shall pass on your concerns to the gentleman himself.'

'Will it be Pierrepoint – he's the usual man, isn't he?'

'That I'm not at liberty to disclose, I'm afraid. Now, is there anything else?'

'Will you be there?'

'I shall, of course.'

'Good. Now there is another thing. Madame Tussauds are putting up a waxwork of me in their Chamber of Horrors. They've asked if someone can come in and take a life mask tomorrow. Would that be alright as a last request?'

Major Benke's expression hadn't changed. He gazed out of the window at the treetops waving over the outer wall and wondered if they weren't all in a madhouse. 'I don't see why not, to be honest. How long would it take?'

'They tell me about three hours.'

'Good God, does it take that long?'

'Well, it'll fill up what would otherwise be a long afternoon. I shan't be able to smile for that long, that's for sure, and so posterity is going to see me looking very serious. I've given Somerfield strict instructions as to what I want to be wearing and I'd be grateful that he's given full co-operation in getting the clothes over to them as soon as possible after Wednesday – *on* Wednesday, if possible.'

'Before I go, Haigh, I should like to thank you on behalf of all of us here as to the way you have conducted yourself. We know it can't be easy and it's made it less of an ordeal for us as well. Thank you.'

The two rose and once again shook hands. 'See you on Wednesday for the performance – get a good seat,' said John.

Next morning, as agreed, Mr Bernard Tussaud, the great-grandson of the founder of the museum, arrived at the suite to start the long process of making a life mask. It demanded a lot of patience from his subject as layer after layer of plastering was wrapped around his face until he was unable to see and only able to breathe through straws poked through the plaster into his mouth. The cast would eventually be taken back to the museum and filled with molten wax until it set, after which the cast would be removed. The carefully chosen eyeballs would be inserted from inside the mould into the sockets, and hair, eyebrows and moustache added hair by hair. At times during the moulding as it became harder to move and breathe, Haigh joked that Tussaud was going to achieve what the hangman was detailed to do the next morning.

At last the work was complete, to the satisfaction of the artist as well as the subject, and John wondered how many friends would come in one day to look at the finished work. He checked again with Tussaud exactly what he would be wearing and made sure the warders understood as well.

While all this was going on a further but unseen visitor slipped in by a back door to the prison to prepare and carry out his duties for the following morning. Albert Pierrepoint had been hired by the Home Office to carry out the execution with an assistant, and they, as was required, arrived at the prison on the afternoon before the execution to prepare the gallows and measure the drop. This requirement to come in early and spend the night in the prison had put an end to executioners drinking excessively the night before and then bungling the job the next morning because they were still drunk, as in former days. They were allowed a modest but prescribed amount of alcohol, as was the prisoner, but no more.

But John Haigh was now plastered in a different sense, which allowed Pierrepoint the opportunity to have a good look at him through the cell door spyhole and calculate the sort of drop that was necessary for a professional job: too much rope could, and had, resulted in decapitating the prisoner, while too short a drop could mean the spine was not broken and so the prisoner strangled to death. Calculating the drop correctly meant a more humane death, with a sandbag used as a dummy weight beforehand to test the rope and then let it stretch overnight.

Albert Pierrepoint, Britain's most famous executioner, made it a rule not to talk to his victims but to get on with it and dispatch them as quickly and with as much dignity as possible. One of the few exceptions in his career was a prisoner he recognised after looking through the spyhole as an old friend – someone he'd sung duets with back home in the pub. On this occasion he did allow some words of comfort to his friend, who seemed grateful Pierrepoint was doing the job and able to be with him in these last few moments. Another human touch was shown when Pierrepoint was chosen to hang the Nazi war criminals after the Nuremberg trials. He selected Irma Grese, known as the

Beast of Belsen for her especially sadistic treatment of prisoners, to be first of the eleven scheduled that day as she was the youngest – only 22 – and so would probably suffer the most waiting her turn.

John Haigh finished his last day on earth by writing the short note to Stafford Somerfield, and then a last letter to his parents:

9 .8 .1949

My dearest Mum and Dad,

Thank you for your very touching letters which I received this morning and which as you say I suppose will be the last. I shall treasure them and their sentiments so long as consciousness permits.

He then started to look back at his childhood with them:

I hardly need tell you that although I found the early theological restrictions oppressive, there was much that was very lovely.

There was great – in fact, overwhelming – kindness and consideration which I remember with much gratitude.

In these later years, I looked forward with great eagerness to my periodic visits of short duration. How can I possibly tell you how I feel about it and expect you to understand? The richness of anticipation and the pleasure of deciding what I should bring for you and the great joy of presenting it and witnessing the fondness of your reception of it.

Of how when I used to leave I used to wish I was just arriving and yet knowing that I should not have wholly enjoyed a protracted stay. But, like yours, my memoirs are of the very pleasant days. I used to love the walks with dad and the nocturnal chats with mam. How glad I am that I was able to get along last November. I looked forward to that for a whole year.

I do understand what you will feel like in the remaining days ahead and it does grieve me that I shall be unable to share them with you; but we cannot change in the inscrutable predictions of the Eternal. I feel sure that I

shall be near you however from time to time. I, that is my
spirit, shall remain earthbound for some time: my mission
is not yet fulfilled.

Of course, if I were to write to you of my thoughts I
should need a book - or more. Mr Somerfield came again this
afternoon and we had a very pleasant half hour. He will
be collecting my goods and chattels from Eagle and from
the Yard and will in due course be bringing them to you.

I hope you enjoy the Philips Radio. I found it very
satisfactory without interference used with the earth.
There is a built-in aerial as well as the plug for an
outside one - naturally the latter is in storage. You can
get America direct towards the left hand side of the short
wave band in the evening.

My typewriter I know you will not use and this with its
accessories I have asked Somerfield to take to Ba. You will
have heard from the Chaplain in due course. He has spent
at least an hour with me each evening and we have had very
pleasant chats together. You will remember him sending
Christmas cards after I left Dartmoor.

He was very touched by your recent letters. I have no
doubt that should he ever come to Leeds he will come to
see you. Please give my love to everybody and thank them
on my behalf for their kindly solicitations.

To you, each of you, all my love and deep gratitude
for all your loving kindness. May your God of all loving
kindness be very kind to you and heal your sore.

Goodbye, Your loving son, John George.

In fact this wasn't quite the last word to his parents. After his regular, but last,
full meeting with the chaplain, John, with less than twelve hours before his
execution, added a brief postscript:

9.30 p.m. The Chaplain has had a very beautiful note
from Hugh N. Norton (Cathedral) who writes to have the
privilege of consoling with: I have told the Chaplain that
I am sure you will appreciate this. Sonnie.

40

At about 8.30 p.m. the Reverend Baden Ball called on John for his last full meeting. He made it this late because he wanted to make it the last of his rounds to give John as much time as he needed or, if it came to it, as little as he needed. He'd known John since his Dartmoor days when he was then chaplain of the prison and John was serving four years for fraud, for posing as a solicitor in Guildford.

The two men had become friends and exchanged Christmas cards since Dartmoor, and so it was a matter of shock and regret that John was now back in Ball's present patch at Wandsworth, facing execution; his visit was tinged with guilt that whatever he'd said to John in those early days apparently had little effect.

While Ball had distanced himself from most condemned prisoners who'd come into his charge at Wandsworth, with John this was quite impossible. He liked John and counted him as a real friend, misguided perhaps but still a friend. He seemed to be liked by everybody, including the governor and his staff, and for all he knew, he would turn his charm on his executioner in the morning if he got the chance.

As usual the pair shook hands and John motioned a hand towards the chair on the other side of his table with the same courtesy a solicitor might extend to a client.

'How are you?' Ball asked.

'Well, thank you. I've just finished writing to the parents.'

'Talking of letters, John, I've just received one from Hugh Norton at Wakefield Cathedral saying how fondly they remember you and your time at the cathedral.'

'That's very kind. I will pass that on to my parents.'

There was a pause in the conversation while both men thought of all the things they'd wanted to say and now seemed quite unable to.

'I wondered if you'd like to take part in any sort of celebration of communion, perhaps?' asked Ball.

'Sort of last rites, do you mean? I don't think so, I'm probably beyond redemption and any form of forgiveness.'

'Now that I can't agree with that, John – you are never beyond forgiveness in the eyes of God, that's the wonderful thing about Him.'

'You see, Baden, there's nothing to forgive. I know I've done terrible things but they were to be, I couldn't have done anything different. They used to say in the war if a bullet or bomb had your name on it, well, that was it. I had killer written on me the day I was born.'

'I can't agree with that, either, I'm afraid. Christ died for our sins, otherwise what did they put him up on the cross for?'

One of the warders rustled his newspaper behind them, as if he wanted to say something and then thought better of it. 'They put Him on the cross because he was a heretic, like me. Doesn't it occur to you that whatever we say in this country about freedom of speech and worship, we still execute our heretics?' asked John.

'Very well, then, but if you'd like to make confession I'd be glad to hear it – if it would help, of course.'

John gave a short laugh. 'My dear Baden, I think I've confessed enough to the police. There's nothing more to confess unless you want me to make it up. I said to the police they'd never believe it all. I asked the same question of Somerfield and he can't believe it. I live under the Principle, and this dictates what's happened and what will happen tomorrow.'

The warder stopped rustling his newspaper and went back to reading the sports page. 'You see, I don't want to sound ungrateful about your kind offers, and I could of course go through with them, but the one thing I did agree with my parents and my rather odd upbringing is that I don't believe in all this worship business. After all, if I was God I wouldn't expect everything I'd created to go down on its knees and worship me. I'd say, I've made you, I've wound you up with enough to get through life, and get out there and live it.'

'So no regrets and no fear of now reaching the end?'

'None at all, none at all – it's been a wonderful life and I wouldn't change a thing. As to the end, I shall pass from this into another life. Death is not part of life and is something we can't understand, but instead of being afraid of it I shall thank Mr Pierrepoint tomorrow for taking me over to the other side.'

The Reverend Ball gently shook his head. 'Well, I'm still sorry you weren't given a reprieve.'

'There were three of them, you know, the doctors from the Home Office, and I probably spent more time with them than I did with old Yellowknees. It was probably my fault, I'm sure I over-egged it with the dreams and drinking blood and all that business. William Blake saw a tree in Peckham full of angels and no one said he was mad. One of the doctors was the governor of Broadmoor no less and I suppose if he said I wasn't mad then no one was going to say so. Do you know, right the way through this I thought I'd get into Broadmoor but, like the judge said, just because you kill a lot of people doesn't mean you're mad.'

'Is there anything I can do for you? Would you like me to write to your parents?'

'Yes, please, and tell them how I looked and how I sounded. They'll be feeling the worst out of everyone about all this. Their pride and joy, their blue-eyed boy who was held up to be above all the rest, has blown all that to pieces.'

'I shall see you in the morning – I'll come a bit early.'

'That's very kind of you, having to go through all this yourself.'

Ball stood up, a little unsteadily. 'One of the less appealing aspects of this job, I'm afraid.'

They shook hands. 'I'm sorry it's come to this,' said Ball.

'I'm not. I'm not sure that I'd have wanted to be shut up with a load of lunatics in Broadmoor anyway,' said John, and sat down to write his postscript to his parents.

41

On the morning of his execution John Haigh lay on his cell bed fully dressed. It was 2 a.m. and he might have dozed for a few minutes but he wasn't bothered with sleep – after all, he could sleep as much as he wanted after nine. He'd read a bit of Somerfield's book and drunk tea with the warders every time they made a brew.

The whole charade for John was like a hospital operation. Here he was in his private room with male nurses he didn't really want, bringing him cups of tea and accompanying him to the lavatory. He was allowed visitors, most of whom tactfully avoided talking about the operation now looming in a few hours. No one gave him much of a chance of surviving it. A longer convalescence in Broadmoor Hospital had been ruled out because the governor decided he wasn't a suitable case for treatment.

Instead he would undergo a period of recovery in Madame Tussaud's and think of all the people who would come and see him then. His story, now sitting on the table on seventy-two neatly written pages of foolscap, ready for collection, would be read in the *News of the World* by millions. Someone now might even write a book about him.

He doubted his parents would be getting much sleep. He was glad they hadn't made the journey down to see him in these ghastly clothes. What would happen to the Alvis – he suddenly realised he hadn't made any provision with Somerfield about the car – well, the police had it trussed up in Chelsea Police Station. Perhaps he ought to leave it to that chap who wrote to him saying he'd always wanted a car like that. That's exactly how he'd felt about the Alvis: he'd always wanted one like that. One of the reporters had come up while he was sitting in it outside the hotel, smoking a cigarette and fiddling around with something in the glovebox, and taken a photograph. He'd have liked a copy of the photograph. The something he was fiddling with was the penknife he was making sure would be found if anyone started poking around the car. He'd tell them that was the knife he used to tap blood. But he couldn't remember the colour of the knife when asked by the police.

Barbara was another person who wouldn't be sleeping much either. Poor Barbara, she'd come off badly with all this. But marriage wouldn't have worked with her, just as it didn't work with his first marriage. He was still married when it came to it. At least Barbara wouldn't ever have to sue for a divorce now. That was ridiculous her asking why he hadn't killed her – of course he wouldn't kill her, she hadn't any money. That was putting it a bit crudely, but he wouldn't have, even if she'd found out about him. If she'd found out, she wouldn't have believed it and he'd have told her to keep quiet. She would have kept quiet. Funny thing was, now he'd told her and written to her saying she should forget about him and start a new life, that's exactly what he'd done. Out of sight, out of mind. That's the way it had been through his whole life. That would be a good epitaph.

God, he hadn't thought about that either very much. The judge said he'd be buried in the precincts of the prison. No gravestone, Ball told him in the nicest possible way, no epitaph, just a number recorded in a book somewhere so that if they ever needed to dig him up they would know where to go.

Would it hurt, that was the question? He knew he was going into another life, here or somewhere else, and perhaps he ought to concentrate on that. At least he wasn't being shot by a firing squad – he couldn't imagine facing and trusting any of the prison staff he'd met here to actually aim with any accuracy. At least Pierrepoint knew the job, or we assumed he did. That was another thing: he'd have liked to have met Pierrepoint before the operation. After all, you'd expect to meet your surgeon and chat a little with him about how he expected things to go. There would hardly be time for that tomorrow – it wasn't tomorrow any more, it was today. They could give you an anaesthetic to make it a bit easier, a whiff of gas just to see you through. To be fair, he hadn't given his victims that luxury, but he had made it quick and without warning. Not one of his people had seen it coming. It would be easier if they did it now, in the middle of the night unannounced, truss him up and bundle him off quick as you like with no time to think about it.

That was the cruel thing about it; it was going to happen on the stroke of nine, not a minute later and not a minute before, and there was nothing he could do about it. Goering had smuggled a pill into his cell. That was the coward's way out. Pierrepoint never got his hands on him. Pierrepoint would be asleep now, with his alarm set. Even doing this indoors in the safety of the prison was a bit cowardly. They should do it out of doors, in public, even if it was raining, and he could make a last speech about how things stood in the world and how we were all ruled by the Principle, who in turn ruled our very Being, which in turn …

Suddenly people were walking around the cell, talking and banging cups of tea. One of the warders was smiling and asking him if he'd enjoyed his lie in. John looked at his watch – it was eight o'clock. He must have slept because he'd been dreaming. He'd been dreaming about being in the cathedral choir and singing something he couldn't remember. Perhaps this was his life rushing before him. Perhaps they'd already done it.

'Cup of tea for you, John,' said one of the warders, like his mum used to when she woke him up for choir.

'I'd like a bath, please,' he asked, after managing some breakfast.

They said he could have a shower but not a bath because there wasn't time and they took him down the corridor to the bathroom, where he stood naked under the shower and realised that soon he'd be naked again with people poking at him and making sure he was dead and those sorts of things. Still, this doing something now was helping, even if it was only having a shower. He dried and dressed again.

When they got back to the cell the Reverend Ball was there looking very serious and dressed up in his robes, with the Bible in his hand. He reminded John of Judge Humphreys in his long robes and with his serious expression. He wasn't paying any attention to the time now because he wanted to keep doing something, so he made his bed, brushed his hair and helped the warders tidy up his things. He told them all again about what was going to Somerfield and which books were going back to the prison library and generally fussed around until Ball put his hand on his shoulder and suggested they pray together.

Both chaplain and prisoner got down on their knees and prayed for anything that came into Ball's head, but it all went in one ear and came out the other for John because he couldn't take a word in, except to think about his parents and even Barbara, who was probably on her way to work as it was coming up to nine o'clock.

Then the governor came in and, in a kindly way, asked him how he was. He produced a bottle of brandy and suggested he sit down and have a drink.

Then things happened.

There was a tap on his shoulder and he realised someone had come in behind him through the second door, the door no one used. He stood up, turned round and saw it must be the man he'd thought a lot about in the last few hours. 'Ah, Mr Pierrepoint, I've always wanted to meet you,' said John, sticking out a hand.

Pierrepoint took his hand, swung him round and bound it to the other at the wrists behind his back in a leather strap. It was quick but not unkind. John found himself trusting Pierrepoint, the way you would your surgeon before an operation.

'Follow me, please,' said Pierrepoint in a matter-of-fact way, and John followed him through the second door with his assistant behind him and the governor and chaplain behind them. He could see past Pierrepoint to a wooden floor in the next room and a rope noose suspended over the floor. Pierrepoint showed him where to stand on a chalk cross on the wooden trap and John could feel his legs being bound from behind. His two warders stood either side of him on planking over the trap. Pierrepoint looked straight at him, face to face, blue eyes on blue eyes, in a steady gaze that calmed him. He tapped John on the shoulder as if to reassure him and John smiled at him. The steady blue eyes of Pierrepoint was the last thing he saw, as the executioner next fitted a white linen hood over John's face, placed the noose over his head and drew down the leather thong to secure it around the neck, placing the thong under the left ear and tightening the noose. Pierrepoint then stepped back two paces, removed the safety pin on the metal lever and pulled the lever towards him, like a signalman changing the points. The trap opened with a clatter and the bundle on the end of its rope – for now it was no more than a bundle, bound hand and foot with a white mask instead of a face – fell out of sight through the open trap.

The whole operation, from cell to drop, had taken eleven seconds.

42

John Haigh needn't have worried about Pierrepoint getting the calculation on the drop right. The jury at the inquest the next day found that death was due to his neck being dislocated, resulting in damage to the spinal cord and instantaneous death. Otherwise, said the pathologist, he was a healthy man.

Albert Pierrepoint calculated the length of the drop to the nearest inch, 7ft 4in in this case. After execution a further measurement was taken from the level of the gallows floor 'to the heels of the suspended culprit', as the meticulous notes put it, at 7ft 5.5in. The Record of Execution, signed by Pierrepoint and his assistant, Harry Kirk, put John's height at 5ft 8in and his weight at 150lbs.

The rules and regulations surrounding executions were carefully laid down by the prison commissioners and little was left to chance for a bungled hanging, where the miscalculation of the drop could result in distress for both executioners and culprit.

A Prison Commissioners' Memorandum of Execution laid down certain rules of procedure, to include:

1. Trap doors to be stained dark colour and outer edges defined by a white line 3 inches broad painted round the edge of the pit outside the traps
2. The culprit's hands to be bound
3. A white linen cap to be fitted over the head of the culprit
4. The noose to be fitted and kept tight by a stiff leather washer
5. The culprit's legs to be strapped
6. The executioner withdraws the safety pin and pulls the lever which lets down the trap doors
7. Culprit to hang for one hour before being cut down

There were also directions for the executioners to arrive at the prison by 4 p.m. on the afternoon before the execution and then to stay inside the prison until their duties were completed the next day. They were to be provided with accommodation in the prison away from and out of sight from other prisoners. The idea was not simply to break with the old tradition of over-indulgence in alcohol but to go through a series of tests with sandbags of the strength of the rope and calculation of the drop and allowing the rope to stretch overnight. The executioners were then to be up at 6 a.m. the next morning to allow time to complete preparations.

Further provision was made for prison routine to go on very much as normal, although the prisoner should not be able to hear preparations going on next door for the execution, and the prison commission similarly did not want other prisoners to hear the trap opening on the day. Working parties should be kept as far away from the execution area as possible, and younger offenders who might be upset with the approach of the execution were to be identified and given assistance, although what that assistance might be was not mentioned.

The prison chaplain didn't escape regulation either, and in a circular in July 1939 from the prison commission, it was laid down he should co-sign the declaration of judgement of death. The chaplain was given the freedom to walk ahead or behind the prisoner from the condemned cell to the scaffold, and prayers generally with the prisoner were at the chaplain's discretion. However, there were to be no audible prayers once the party had left the cell, although presumably silent prayer was permissible. When it came to the burial later in the prison precincts, it was suggested that a shortened form of the burial service was appropriate, and that the chaplain should robe for the ceremony behind a screen erected at the graveside.

As to the burial, instructions followed the prisoner literally to the grave. All clothing, with exception of the shirt or similar garment, was to be removed from the body, which was to be placed in a coffin made of half-inch wood, deal or pine. Sides of the coffin were to be well perforated with large holes. Lime was not to be used. The grave was to be dug 8–10ft deep and the coffin, once placed, was to be covered with 1ft of earth and then 3in of charcoal. Further coffins could be laid in the same grave at a later date, using available sites in sequence, but not until after seven years. The coffin, however, was not to be less than 4ft below ground level.

A further and thoughtful provision was that the prison clock chime be disconnected, although exactly when was left to the discretion of the prison governor, and whether this was with the condemned prisoner or the rest of the inmates in mind, or both, was not stated.

Finally it was the task of the governor and medical officer to complete a form of satisfaction questionnaire as to the performance of the executioners. They were to confirm that the executioners performed their duties satisfactorily, that their general demeanour during their period in the prison was satisfactory, that they'd shown merit and physical suitability for the post and that there was no reason to suppose they would bring discredit to the post by lecturing or giving interviews. The last box to be ticked was the standard question to complete an employer's questionnaire: would you employ these people again?

Albert Pierrepoint and his assistant received full marks for their performance in this instance, and the pathologist for the inquest found that John Haigh's stomach contained the residue of a recent meal with a faint smell of alcohol, perhaps a brandy at the end to see him through the ordeal. His 'generative organs' were healthy with no venereal disease, with further confirmation that death was instantaneous.

A prison note on 1 September 1949 shows that the only property left by John Haigh was a pair of cufflinks and £2 odd in cash. This was sent to his father as next of kin. John wore a grey suit on the day he was hanged, with his green suit being sent to 'the newspaper people' to be delivered to Madame Tussauds.

The grey suit worn at the time of execution was prison property and accordingly recycled for further use.

43

Otherwise, in the hours and days following the execution, it was a case of 'Haigh is Dead – Long Live Haigh'. The usual certificates of death were posted on the main gates of Wandsworth prison, one signed by the sheriff and the other by the prison surgeon, stating he had examined 'the Body of John George Haigh on whom Judgment of Death was this day executed in the said Prison; and that on that Examination I found that the said John George Haigh was dead'.

A large crowd had gathered outside the prison gates to await confirmation of the execution, mostly women and a large number of children joining in the holiday atmosphere. But the persons who were going to keep the Haigh story alive, and indeed had the strongest financial incentive to keep the story alive, were Stafford Somerfield and his team on the *News of the World*.

As promised, Somerfield took the jacket and trousers, green socks and red tie that John had worn for the committal proceedings at Horsham Magistrates Court over to Madame Tussauds in Marylebone. The wax effigy of John, back in his own clothes, looked dapper as usual and rather younger than the fortieth birthday reached shortly before his death, but without his usual smile. Nevertheless he was in his new home along with housemates Burke and Hare, Dr Crippen, Marie Antoinette and other victims of the French Revolution. The last time he had been there was with Barbara, shortly before his arrest, when he could still smile.

'John George Haigh's Own Story' started to be serialised in the *News of the World* on Sunday, 31 July 1949, eleven days before the execution date and with the only chance of a reprieve in the hands of the Home Secretary and his doctors. The 'confession', as it was referred to by the newspaper, started with a list in John's longhand of his nine victims with their various methods of disposal, to include comments like 'cut neck/sucked blood'. This constant reference to blood was prominent in the story from the start, with John describing his mother as a great student of dreams and how they foretold the future, and how John himself started having dreams of Christ with blood pouring from his wounds after he started in the choir of Wakefield Cathedral. He then describes being smacked with a hairbrush on the back of the hand by his mother and the bristles drawing blood, which he sucked off and found the taste agreeable. This incident 'marked the genesis of a destiny'. A car accident added to his lust for blood and then the dreams about the trees turning to crucifixes dripping with blood. This then led to his first murder, that of Donald McSwan.

How much of all this was fact or fiction we don't know, and it has been pointed out that the dreams, not mentioned by John at Lewes prison, were introduced and grew only after John arrived at Brixton. However, the fact is that he stuck to the story to the end, telling Barbara this was his motive for the killings and telling his parents in correspondence at a stage when there wasn't much point in lying. Equally, the truth might have been more prosaic: John simply couldn't face the fact that he had killed these good friends of his because they were wealthy and, as a good forger, he could convert their assets to fund his lifestyle.

Barbara and John's parents looked up to him; he was the clever boyfriend or son, the inventor with brains and a successful lifestyle with a talent and interest in music: someone who knew his way around town. The fact that he might be homosexual, a fraudster and murderer was not the image he wanted to leave behind for posterity. Posh was the image he wanted to create, with bespoke clothes, expensive hotels, luxury cars and upper-class friends. The only way he was going to get into Madame Tussauds was the wrong way, like everything else in his life.

He wrote 'my attitude was one of faith that all would be provided for' and that none of the killings was planned with financial gain in mind. So when he did find out that there was financial gain, to his surprise, then he believed he was being cared for by some supreme force.

Four years after the trial and execution, Dr Henry Yellowlees, still smarting from his mauling at the hands of the prosecution in the trial, wrote a book titled *To Define True Madness* and dealt with the issue of insanity in criminal law. His view was that for a competent modern psychiatrist it was impossible to give a fair picture of any person's state of mind if forced to do so in terms of the M'Naghten Rules. Very often, he believed, it was hard to say if someone was mad enough to be within the M'Naghten Rules. Added to this was the pressure of interrogation from counsel, which sometimes caused an expert witness to lose his head and become dogmatic and irritable, forgetting he is there to help the court in a legal inquiry. Too often, felt Yellowlees, a psychiatric is told he is plain wrong and that his diagnosis is wrong by a lawyer 'who knows no more of psychological medicine than he was been able to acquire the night before'. Very often this is set right by the judge, but one can't rely on this, and matters are not helped by the psychiatrist being labelled 'for the defence', with the prison medical officers as acting for the prosecution. If under the M'Naghten Rules the accused's mental state and his degree of criminal responsibility are to be treated as different things, then the psychiatrist should be regarded as the authority on the mental state and the lawyers left to sort out the question of criminal responsibility.

A difficulty here, said Yellowlees, is that very few patients are really mad enough to come within the M'Naghten Rules and he found Haigh a case in point: as he pointed out in the trial, Haigh was medically mad but not 'M'Naghten mad'. Both the newspapers and public hysteria generally held that the medical evidence was simply a ruse to get Haigh off, and as a result counsel attacked the whole insanity issue rather than dealing solely with the responsibility issue.

In short Dr Yellowlees felt his evidence was dealt with improperly by the court, and that the court was unfriendly and hostile. The irony was that this was the only occasion when he gave evidence in a trial believing the accused *was* criminally responsible but feeling nevertheless his views on Haigh's mental state should be put to the court. However, it was to the credit of Mr Justice Humphreys in the Haigh case, though this is not mentioned by Yellowlees in his book, that in his summing up he instructed the jury they could regard the accused's paranoia as a mental disease for M'Naghten purposes, as on this occasion he did not want this to get in the way of the criminal responsibility issue.

At the end of what he has to say about criminal insanity, Yellowlees refers to the notorious case of John Straffen, who was tried just three years after John Haigh. The author also examined this case in his book *Escape from Broadmoor*, but all that needs saying here is that this was another case where the accused was not mad enough for the M'Naghten Rules. A 'mental defective',

John Straffen spent fifty-seven years in conventional prisons (making him Britain's longest-serving prisoner) after escaping from Broadmoor after only six months and murdering again in the four hours he was at large. This time the doctors decided he wasn't insane, despite such a short stay in Broadmoor, and he was only saved from hanging at the last minute by a reprieve from the Home Secretary, who by then was Sir David Maxwell Fyfe, Haigh's defence barrister.

Others in Straffen's position weren't so lucky, and clearly something had to be done about these cases. The Homicide Act 1957 was passed a few years later introducing Diminished Responsibility as a defence to murder, reducing it to manslaughter. The Act referred to 'an abnormality of mind' rather than a mental disease and allowed the jury a wider interpretation of the medical opinion and whether the accused was 'putting it on' to escape a murder conviction. However, the Act probably wouldn't have saved John Haigh, as it didn't in the more recent case of Peter Sutcliffe, the Yorkshire Ripper, but would have served as a defence for John Straffen and Derek Bentley, the co-defendant in the Bentley and Craig case.

One person who didn't shed tears at John Haigh's execution was his wife Beatrice Hamer, whom he married in 1934 but never divorced despite the marriage lasting barely four months. This story gave the *News of the World* a further scoop when it reported that Albert Pierrepoint received a telegram reading 'Dear Albert – I am getting married today to Mrs John Haigh' on 20 August 1949, ten days after the execution.

Pierrepoint allegedly replied 'Congratulations to you both. Good luck' from the pub Help the Poor Struggler he ran in Oldham, Lancashire. A *News of the World* reporter telephoned the address near Padstow from where the original telegram had apparently been sent and spoke to a Captain Neale, who said:

> It's a damnable hoax. My dear wife is sitting beside me now. We have been happily married for years, and we are still in love; God bless her. Why should we marry a second time? This is a damnable scandal. If anyone breathes one word of scandal about us I will sue them by the first post for £15,000. I know nothing about any telegram. I did not send such a thing.

But the newspaper reported that, according to Albert Pierrepoint, the telegram came from Danny Neale whom he knew as an army officer in the war when Pierrepoint was hanging Nazi criminals after the Nuremberg trials. The *News of the World* added that locals were emphatic that there had been a wedding between Captain Neale and John Haigh's widow and that there was a party in progress at the Neale household. However, in his book *Executioner:*

Pierrepoint Albert retracted all this and said that the telegram was sent by an imposter and Captain Neale brought legal action as a result.

On the question of capital punishment generally, Albert Pierrepoint, looking back in the book on his career, concluded:

> During my time as executioner, I believed with all my heart that I was carrying out a public duty. I conducted each execution with great care and a clear conscience. I never allowed myself to get involved with the death penalty controversy.
>
> I now sincerely hope that no man is ever called upon to carry out another execution in my country. I have come to the conclusion that executions solve nothing, and are only an antiquated relic of a primitive desire for revenge which takes the easy way and hands over the responsibility for revenge to other people.

John Haigh was not the last person to be hanged by Albert Pierrepoint after a trial led by Sir Hartley Shawcross as prosecutor. Sir Hartley remained chief prosecutor for the United Kingdom in the Nuremberg trials until 1949 and was attorney general at the same time, until he briefly became president of the Board of Trade in the Labour government in 1951. After the government's defeat in the same year, he stayed on as an MP until 1958, when he was made one of the first life peers as Baron Shawcross.

Sir David Maxwell Fyfe, after a brief spell himself as attorney general in Churchill's caretaker government, handed over the office to Sir Hartley in 1945 on Churchill's defeat. However, he was then appointed as Sir Hartley's deputy in Nuremberg, and while Sir Hartley took more of a back seat in the prosecution of the war criminals, Sir David was actively involved on a day-to-day basis and conducted a particularly effective cross-examination of Hermann Goering. With the return of a Conservative government in 1951, Churchill made Maxwell Fyfe Home Secretary; he became notorious for refusing a reprieve to Derek Bentley who, like John Straffen, had a mental age of 11 and received wide support from MPs and the public alike for a reprieve. In 1954 he became Lord Chancellor as Lord Kilmuir, a post he held for eight years until Harold MacMillan's famous Night of the Long Knives.

Dr Keith Simpson, the pathologist who painstakingly sifted through the soil in Leopold Road to find and identify Mrs Durand-Deacon's gallstones and bones, went on to become one of the country's leading pathologists, with a list of cases that sounded like a *Who's Who* of British post-war murders, including John Christie, Dr John Bodkin Adams, James Hanratty, the Kray brothers, Lord Lucan and Roberto Calvi ('God's Banker' in the Vatican who was found hanging underneath Blackfriars Bridge). He was a keen advocate for legalising abortion and once said he saw at least two young girls a week in post mortems as a result of septic abortion before it was legalised.

Sir Walter Monckton, who had successfully handled the application for contempt against the *Daily Mirror*, went on to become Minister of Labour when Churchill came back to power in 1951. When Monckton became Anthony Eden's Minister of Defence in 1955, he was the only member of Eden's Cabinet to oppose his Suez policy and was moved to Paymaster General. It was even on the cards for him to become Lord Chief Justice, but in 1957 he instead chose to join the board of the Midland Bank.

Forty years later, Barbara Stephens, John Haigh's constant and faithful companion for five years, remembered him as a charming man, a very pleasant character and a most attractive personality. There was never a hint of what he was up to and it was only later that she realised he needed psychiatric help. She remained convinced he would have disposed of her had he needed to, and that the dreams and the blood drinking were all made up. She married some years later, but it didn't last and she divorced with a poor opinion of men. Her worst time was between John's sentencing and execution, and it was a great relief when it was all over. She still thought execution was the best thing in the circumstances and remained in favour of capital punishment. For John, she felt, it was the best thing that could have happened.

Sir Travers Humphreys, the trial judge who gave that 'masterly' summing up to the jury, retired as the senior and oldest King's Bench judge in 1951. On his wife's death in 1953, he moved into the Onslow Court Hotel, the former residence of John Haigh and Mrs Durand-Deacon.

He wouldn't have needed much of an introduction to the hotel after meeting the manager, Mrs Robbie, and her book-keeper, Mrs Kirkwood, as witnesses in John Haigh's trial, when he was informed of the rates for different rooms on the first and fourth floors, the seating arrangements in the dining room and given a glimpse of the lives of some of the residents, to include the late Mrs Durand-Deacon, Mrs Constance Lane and John Haigh himself.

Sadly Sir Travers only enjoyed a year there before his death in 1954, but his judge's pension should have allowed him a decent room on the first floor, perhaps Room 115, once occupied by Olive Durand-Deacon. Perhaps there would have been times when he was having a meal in the dining room or a coffee in the Tudor Room when he saw a figure with a neat moustache and carefully oiled hair, dressed smartly in a Savile Row suit, offer another guest the chance to buy jewellery, a handbag, or even clothing from a suitcase he'd just acquired – really an opportunity not to be missed – and give his good friend Sir Travers a smile and a wink with those bright blue eyes.

Bibliography

Briffet, D., *The Acid Bath Murders* (West Sussex, Field Place Press, 1988)

Dunboyne, Lord (ed.), *The Trial of John George Haigh* (London, William Hodge, 1953)

Firmin, S., *Crime Man* (London, Hutchinson, 1950)

Humphreys, Sir T., *A Book of Trials* (London, William Heinemann, 1953)

La Bern, A., *Haigh – The Mind of a Murderer* (London, W.H. Allen, 1973)

Lowe, G., *Escape From Broadmoor* (Stroud, The History Press, 2013)

Pierrepoint, A., *Pierrepoint: Executioner* (London, George G Harrap, 1974)

Somerfield, S., *Haigh* (Manchester, Hood Pearson, 1950)

Yellowlees, Dr H., *To Define True Madness* (London, Penguin, 1953)

Index